Geneal on the Macintosh

David Tippey

Printed in England by Parchment (Oxford) Ltd

Distributed by Family Tree Magazine
61 Great Whyte, Ramsey, Huntingdon, Cambridgeshire PE17 1HL
Phone 01487 814050, fax 01487 711361

Published in 1996 by David Hawgood
26 Cloister Road, Acton, London W3 0DE

ISBN 0 948151 13 7

Contents

Chapter 1. Hardware and Software
What equipment and programs do you need?

Why the Apple Macintosh Computer?

The PC is the most commonly used general purpose computer in both home and office, being widely available at affordable prices, mainly because the Apple Macintosh was seen, until recently, as the foremost machine for desk top publishing and an expensive graphics orientated computer. Home owners were few, and it was used mainly by printers and drawing studios. However Macs are now readily available in High Street Stores. Apple are now about the third largest computer manufacturer worldwide, although Macs represented only 15% of the UK market in 1995. Other makers are now producing Power Macintosh machines under license and PC companies like IBM are interested in putting Mac operating systems with their machines. Prices of Macs are more compatible with PCs than a few years ago, and one of the best kept secrets of the computer world is out; the Macintosh computer has an operating system which makes it really easy to use!

For years, whilst PC users battled with reluctant DOS operating systems and the semi user friendly Windows, Apple users have had an easily understood desktop and filing cabinet style interface, hiding the horrors and mysteries of the operating system from the user. Amongst other attributes, the simple handling of documents and files, coupled with the ability to use sensible names for your documents, makes the Mac superbly simple to use. Windows was a big improvement on DOS, and the much hyped Windows 95 was supposed to bestow the same advantages long enjoyed by the Macintosh user, but many buyers found it didn't quite deliver the goods.

A survey by the Gartner Group in America showed that companies who used Apple Mac computers spent considerably less on staff training and repairs than companies using PCs. The saving of about 25% was because Macs are easier to set up and maintain and staff training could focus on the use of the programs not the computer.

So for the family historian who doesn't want to spend all their time learning to use a computer, or is basically "technology shy", the Apple Mac is a fairly painless introduction to a machine which will help make family history research an easier and more rewarding pastime.

Why use a computer?

If you are new to family history research, you will probably not have collected too much information yet. If you are a tidy, methodical worker your data so far is probably neatly written in a notebook or on record sheets. It is still fairly easy to consult by flicking through the pages or laying out the records on a table. One of the problems with research is that you rapidly accumulate information, some directly connected and some which may be useful at a later date. As your family tree grows so does your pile of records, certificates and notes, and it gets much slower and more difficult to retrieve the information you know you have "somewhere", but which might be the link you are after. If you record your data on the backs of envelopes and library leaflets, you will probably start to come unstuck after the first couple of family groups and you will have no chance with a family tree of 800 people!

I am fairly untidy by nature, very much a "notes on envelopes" man, and there was no way I could successfully struggle through mountains of paper to compile my family tree. Buying a computer was the "shove in the back" to get on with the task I had only thought about doing for the previous 10 years. Of course by then it was too late and the last of my father's generation had died, making my task even more difficult, but that is another story.

Computers are constructed to cope with organisational tasks for you; they are extremely good at data storage, searching and printing out the information for you, all these facilities are a great help in constructing and presenting your family history from the snippets of information gathered in your research. Using a computer will tend to help you become more organised and methodical too.

Even older slower machines can sort through hundreds of your ancestors records, to find the right 'John Peters born in Stockton in 1853', before you could find the first couple of John's on your record sheets. With the right programs they will draw family trees and produce written reports from your family data, faster than you can get your pen to paper too! They definitely help you get more out of your hobby and enable you to present your data professionally for viewing by the rest of the family. When you have "finished" your research you will also have the ideal tool to write that family history you were thinking about.

Which Macintosh?

Although prices of computers have plummeted, especially in terms of what you get for your money, they still represent a fairly hefty cash outlay, so you need to try and determine just what you need from your machine. The problem with this is that until you have owned and used one, it is very difficult to appreciate just what you can to do with a computer. However the demands of the many family historians will probably be satisfied by a fairly basic machine, which will work as a word processor and happily run specialist Family History and ordinary database programs. You may eventually be seduced into scanning, storing and editing pictures and working with video of course, and then you will need to buy something more powerful.

The Apple machine range has recently changed, virtually all models are now Power Macs; this is a new faster, more powerful series of processor chips, roughly equivalent to the PC Pentium chips. Unlike PC manufacturers, who still build the non-Pentium machines, Apple have dropped the older, slower machines from the range completely, which means that many of these computers are available second-hand at very reasonable prices, as companies and individuals upgrade their equipment. The last two machines I have bought were out of production within six months of my purchasing them, but out of current production doesn't make them obsolete, both work perfectly well, my local dealer can still repair much older machines than mine, and you can still add extras such as scanners, CD ROM drives and modems.

Buying second-hand is a bit like buying a car, I wouldn't buy from the classified section of my local paper, you pay a bit more at the dealer's, but you should get a warranty included, and you have someone to turn to if you need help.

It is always good advice to buy the most powerful, fully featured set up you can afford, but like cars, basic computers will still get there in the end, just not as fast. For basic family history work, look for at least 2Mb RAM (working memory), 40Mb Hard disk (program and file storage) and make sure that the machine is running Operating System 7 or above, so that your choice of programs isn't limited. Such a set-up will cope with most family history tasks except drawing very large charts or handling large graphics files containing photographs. As long as you are not impatient by nature, more RAM and more hard disk storage, are generally more useful than extra speed. Many of Apple's range over the last few years will fit the bill and you should be able to buy a machine suitable for genealogy with a keyboard and monitor for less than £500. Look out for these models (listed in order of speed) : -
Classic (built in B&W monitor), or these models with colour monitors : Colour Classic (monitor built in), LC, Performa 200, LCll, Performa 400, LClll, Performa 450 (all with separate monitors).

I use two machines, my old Classic 4/40 (4Mb RAM and 40 MB hard disk), which is very neat and compact, almost a portable, has a built in B&W monitor of exceptional clarity and is a little slow when working with large files, but fast enough for general work.

My other machine is an LClll 8/80, faster than my Classic, but still slow when compared to the new Power Macs! It will search databases fast enough and do all the tasks I ask of it, although it's speed definitely lets it down when I try to work on a pedigree chart that covers 54 A4 pages, but what would I do with all those pieces of paper anyway?

In addition I have a Stylewriter B&W inkjet printer, and a small hand scanner for inputting photographs and documents. A very humble set up by today's all singing and dancing, Audio Visual machine capabilities, but adequate for my needs for the present.

If you want a faster, more powerful machine, capable of drawing very large trees, or ones including a lot of photographs, or want to use it for enhancing and retouching large numbers of family photographs then look out for an LC / Performa 475, Centris or Quadra machine or better still go for one of the new Power Macs.

A Printer

The one essential item you need to go with the basic computer, keyboard and monitor, is a printer. Printers have more mechanical parts to wear and cause problems, so I am not very keen on second-hand ones. Dot matrix printers are noisy and the output from the cheaper printers is often very poor, their principal use these days is for businesses, printing multiple part forms such as invoices/delivery notes etc. Ink jet or bubble jet printers are much quieter and give you a print quality almost equal to that in books and magazines, for little more than a dot matrix machine. The results are not quite as good as laser printers and print quality very much depends on the type of paper used, but my Apple Stylewriter ll in "Best quality " mode using good quality ink jet paper, will print masters suitable for photocopying to produce a small run of booklets, showing very little loss in print quality. If you want to use colour in your charts and documents, colour ink jet printers are not too expensive either and the latest 720dpi ones from Epson produce a very good quality result.

Ink jet cartridges are rather expensive, because with most makes you are buying a new print-head with each cartridge. They don't wear out that fast though, so it is more economical to buy a cartridge re-fill kit or have them re-filled by one of the specialist companies who advertise in the computer magazines.

Programs

You will of course need one or more programs to run on your computer, without them it is little more than an ornament. If you are lucky in the purchase of a second-hand machine, it may come with various programs, but make sure that you get the original program disks and the manuals too. Without owning the original disks to the program, which usually have the serial number on them, you may be infringing the program licence if you use it, ie committing software piracy! Later machines came with some software pre-loaded, these usually have a registration document and a manual, make sure you get these.

The first program you will probably think of buying, is a specialist family history database program, however it is possible to work without one, using word processor, database, spreadsheet and drawing packages, to record and present all your information. Many Macs have recently been sold with Claris Works, an integrated package containing effectively 6 programs, which are all fully compatible with each other ; a word processor, database, spreadsheet, drawing, painting and communications package. Various other software companies have written similar integrated packages, Microsoft Works being one of the most common. One of these integrated packages will probably give you all the additional features you need to complement a genealogy database program, unless you want to handle pictures. The use of these integrated packages in genealogy is discussed in the next chapter.

Chapter 2 : Genealogy using non specialist programs

Integrated packages?

Integrated packages are ideal for the home user and represent very good value. The facilities are usually rather less than are included in a set of stand-alone professional packages, but adequate for most work. Having said that, each new version that comes out, brings with it a greater range of functions, and they are no longer the cost conscious compromise that they were. Claris Works 4.0 for instance, now includes excellent desk top publishing functions, which would enable you to put together a very professional family newsletter, or design and print your own family history book. The trade-off is, that as programs get more functions added they get larger and take up more of your hard disk space and need more RAM to work with. If you bought a second-hand machine with an early version of Claris or Microsoft Works, then providing you have the original disks or registration documents you will be able to upgrade to the latest fully featured version quite cheaply. The programs that are bundled with new computers are often older versions, and you have to buy the upgrade if you want the latest facilities.

The following section will discuss how the various functions of the integrated package, or those of equivalent individual programs, can be utilised for Family history research.

Word-processor

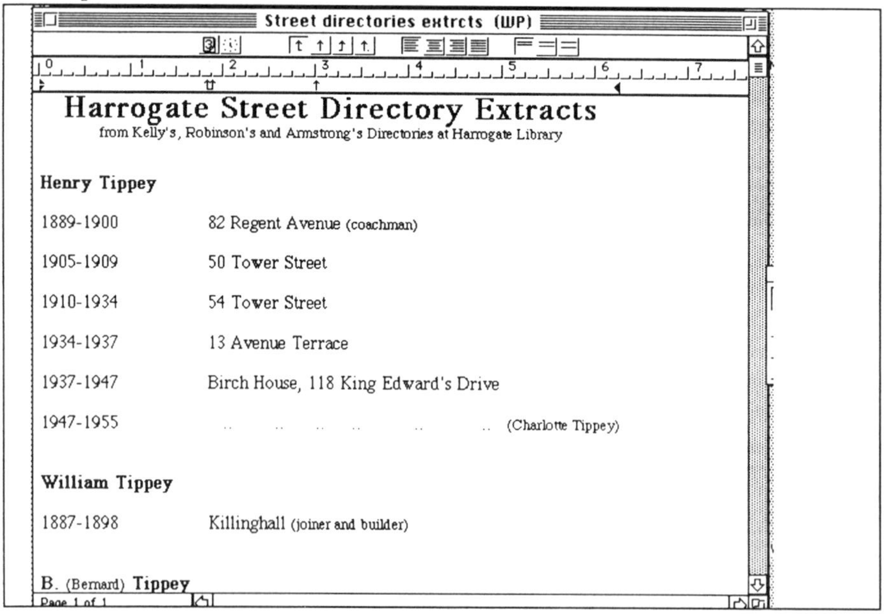

Figure 1. Amongst other jobs, the wordprocessor can be used to keep tidy updateable lists of information and searches, as well as being used for the usual correspondence etc.

Register Report - 18 February 1996

First Generation

1.
Mary Tipping - 151.

29 January 1768 Sarah, daughter of Mary Tipping, illegitimate St.

There are various Tipping/Tippin entries around the York Area, and the following information is from various YPRS transcripts and Poll Books:

Richard Tipping, which is spelt Tippin on the marriage register entry, could possibly her brother, and was shown as a York Butcher in the Shambles in the Poll book for 1774[5] . He married Sussanah Moyser of St Helens (Lancs. town or parish?)on15 Dec 1763 at Holy Trinity, King's Court, York. They had several children baptised at Holy Trinity church [6] :
John bpt. 3 Sept 1766
Thomas bpt. 17 Oct 1769
Mary bpt. 29 Dec 1772
Ann bpt. 16 Oct 1774
He died between 1774 and 1779 and his widow re-married to Robert Todd of Dunnington on the 27 June 1779[6]
A Richard Tipping is listed as a cordwainer in Walmgate in the 1758 Poll book, possibly the same person or a relation, possibly father.

She had the following children:

2 i. Sarah Tippy - 157 (Illegitimate)

Second Generation

---

2. Sarah Tippy - 157. Born 1768 in York. Christen 29 January 1768 in St Michael-le-Belfry, York. Died 1861 in Roecliffe. Buried in St Mary, Roecliffe.

Baptised at St Michael le Belfry , York,
Entry reads : 29 January 1768, Sarah Tippy, daughter of Mary Tipping, illegitimate)[7]
She had lived in Roecliffe, nr Boroughbridge from at least 1841, as she is listed there in the 1841-61 census, but probably before that, as her son Joseph was a Brick and Tile maker in York and Roecliffe had a brick works and tile sheds, where he may have worked first (He would probably have started work around 1822, aged 14). He also gave Roecliffe as his birth place in the 1851 census, (he was baptised in the correct parish to confirm it was definitely this area) which would have put them there in 1808.
Sarah died of "old age" at Roecliffe in 1861 Aged 99 ? (incorrect age) and is buried in Roecliffe churchyard[8]
Date of burial?

1841 census : reads: Sarah Tippey, 75, Spinster, Roecliffe[9]

1851 census : HO 107 2282 fol. 59 obv. : Roecliffe, Sarah Tippey aged 84 born York : head of household: married (all other entries disagree with this)[9]

1861 census : Sarah Tippey, aged 99 formerly Agricultural labourer, Deaf, supported by Great Ouseburn Union, living at the home of George Slater, 83yr old farrier and his housekeeper, near the Crown Inn Roecliffe. (her reported age is obviously incorrect by then, as it is quoted as 99 at her burial later the same year too.)[9]

Children:

Figure 2. Some genealogical databases use your word processor program to prepare reports. This example is prepared by Reunion using WriteNow. Once made into a WP file you can edit and re-arrange the layout to suit yourself, even use it as the skeleton of a more narrative family history. Here notes for further research have been added.

The written word has been revolutionised by the word-processor. The facilities for altering or re-arranging blocks of text are a revelation if you have only used a pen or a typewriter before. With the help of the spell-checker and thesaurus, and a grammar checker with some programs, even those of us who failed English miserably at school can pass as reasonably literate.

One of the mainstays of family history research is letter writing, and it is also one of the great pleasures. If you need to write to all the Smiths in the London phonebooks, you can write a master letter and save it as a stationary document. Each time you open the stationary document, a new version of it is created, which you can then edit, personalising the name and possibly the odd sentence too. After printing this letter, say to Albert Smith, you file away it in a folder, go back to your original stationary document and open it as a letter to Bertram Smith etc.

You may want to start writing your family history straight away; the good thing about the computer is that you can go back and add or correct information as you progress, so you can start with a newssheet and end up with the definitive work.

Probably more useful, is to keep more extensive, narrative family group information than is stored in the notes field of your genealogical database. Here you can more safely put all that sensitive family information supplied by aunt Nelly, as you are not likely to unwittingly send it in that GEDCOM transfer to cousin Kate in Australia, whose mother was the subject of the revelations!

The word processor is also very useful for keeping up-datable lists of all manner of things; for instance, all the records or books you have searched through in a particular library or archive, with notes added to say whether they were successful searches and where the extracted information is entered (see Figure 1).

You can with patience, create small family group charts too, although you will probably have to resort to a ruler and pen for some of the connecting lines. Careful setting of the tabs will help you type the information into the correct places, although using a drawing or paint program is much easier.

Organising your files

At this point I will say a little more about the Apple Operating System, this simplifies operations such as file storage and retrieval, making the computer so easy to use. The monitor screen becomes your desktop and, like the real thing, it would be quite easy to create a whole pile of correspondence and leave it littering your desk top as you work. When you close and save each file, you name it (Apple Macs allow you to use real titles, which you can read and understand weeks later, unlike the 8 letter DOS names), and it is then represented by a small picture or icon, with the filename underneath. If you just leave these on your desktop, then just like the real thing, it will become so cluttered that you won't be able to find anything. This is where the filing cabinet analogy comes in. The Mac uses a system of hierarchical folders to enable you to store and find all your documents. You set up a series of folders to organise all your files. A typical example would be to start with a folder called "Family History", when opened this will reveal three folders labelled "Smith's data", "Brown's data" and "Letters". The first two are the family lines you are following and will contain database, spreadsheet and word-processor documents relating to that family, and these could be split up into further folders if necessary. The letter file contains three more folders marked "Smith", "Brown" and "Other" into which the letters are sorted. This way, the vast quantities of files that you end up with, are broken down into small manageable collections under different categories, so that you can easily find just the one you want. There are further provisions to help you organise these individual folders more efficiently. Instead of showing a picture icon for every file, which takes a lot of space and is only suitable where a folder contains a few files, you can list the filenames alphabetically or by the date they were last altered, which is very useful where the folder contains many files. Furthermore it is possible to tag the files with a priority colour code. I tag letters with a red tag when I write them, which keeps them in the top part of the list, awaiting a reply. When I get a letter in return, I will tag the original file with yellow if the reply requires a response from me, or a green tag if it doesn't, thus I can see at a glance who I must write to and whom I am waiting to hear from. Letters that never get a reply are eventually untagged to sink to the bottom of the list, fortunately these are very few.

Spreadsheets

Spreadsheets and databases have functions which overlap somewhat. Spreadsheets are principally designed for working with figures and performing calculations, but can be used to create text lists too. I have used a spreadsheet to organise and display information extracted from the St Catherine's House Indexes of Births, Deaths and Marriages. The spreadsheet in Figure 3 is organised as a series of columns, Surname,

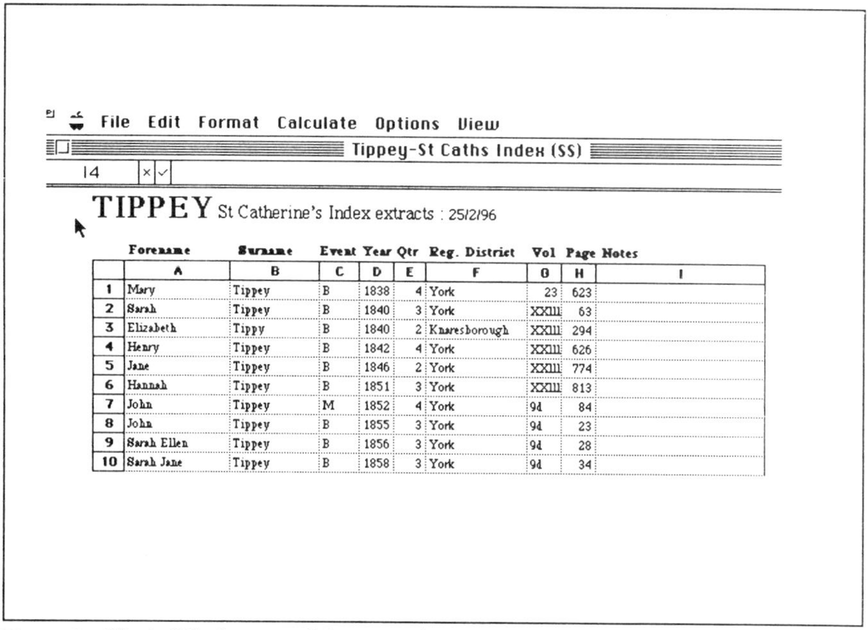

File Edit Format Calculate Options View

Tippey-St Caths Index (SS)

14

TIPPEY St Catherine's Index extracts : 25/2/96

	Forename	Surname	Event	Year	Qtr	Reg. District	Vol	Page	Notes
	A	B	C	D	E	F	G	H	I
1	Mary	Tippey	B	1838	4	York	23	623	
2	Sarah	Tippey	B	1840	3	York	XXIII	63	
3	Elizabeth	Tippy	B	1840	2	Knaresborough	XXIII	294	
4	Henry	Tippey	B	1842	4	York	XXIII	626	
5	Jane	Tippey	B	1846	2	York	XXIII	774	
6	Hannah	Tippey	B	1851	3	York	XXIII	813	
7	John	Tippey	M	1852	4	York	9d	84	
8	John	Tippey	B	1855	3	York	9d	23	
9	Sarah Ellen	Tippey	B	1856	3	York	9d	28	
10	Sarah Jane	Tippey	B	1858	3	York	9d	34	

Figure 3. Claris Works spreadsheet used to store extracts from the St. Catherine's House Indexes.

Christian Name, Year, Quarter etc. Each entry is one line, with the relevent information entered into each column. The entries have been added randomly as I check out various family events, so the SORT function can be used to put them into date order, or alphabetically by Christian name, or into whatever order I want them at the time. These sorted lists can be consulted on the screen or printed copies made when necessary.

Databases

Most spreadsheets are not as flexible as databases though, which are much more useful for storing and sorting all the miscellaneous facts and events, which may fit into your research at a later date, but don't fit now. Databases are designed to handle text and figures, but generally have better sorting and selecting functions, as well as better reporting formats than spreadsheets. Figure 4 shows an example.

Large databases can be built up and entries can be selected and sorted by virtually any criteria, then output in a variety of useful formats. I am working on a one name study of the Woodmanseys, a family whose roots are in East Yorkshire in the area of Beverley, and I have loads of miscellaneous information, downloaded from the IGI, entered from printed MI's, Parish Records and census entries. This is all being stored in a database which can then be searched and sorted to find family groups or particular individuals who fit certain given criteria. Once I have sorted the data into family groups, they can then be added to my main genealogical database, which I don't want clogging up with all the odd individual entries.

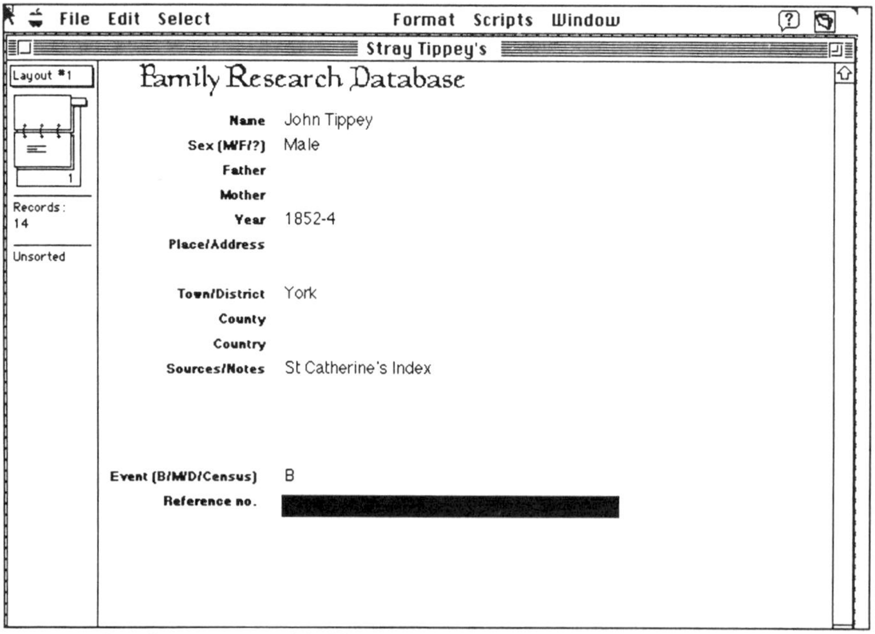

Figure 4. Database set up with Filemaker Pro to keep details of stray entries which don't yet have a known tie to the main family tree which is kept on a specialist genealogical database

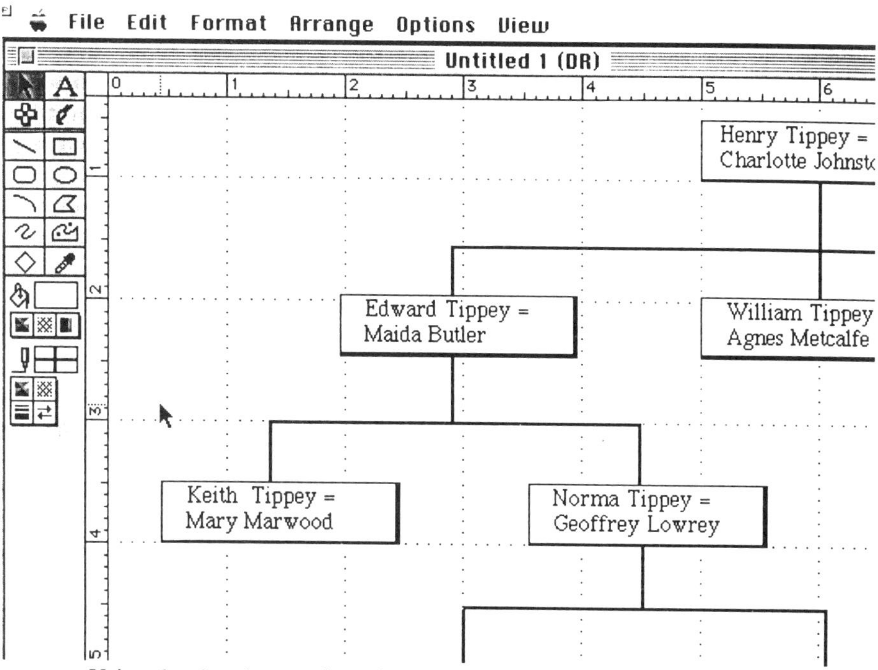

Figure 5. Using the drawing section of Claris Works to prepare a family chart, which can be as simple or complex as you want.

When data is displayed or printed not all facts need to be included, so one large database could be set up to cover the requirements of Census, IGI, St Catherine's Index, and Parish Record information etc., but the sets of data displayed on screen or printed could look as if they were individual databases.

Drawing and Painting programs

When you are ready to create a pedigree chart, draw and paint programs are ideal. Start by creating one for a small family group to get used to the program functions. Information is typed in for each individual as a separate piece of text, and then these blocks of text are dragged around the screen to arrange them. Lines and boxes around the text can then be added easily, especially if the Snap to Grid function is used to make sure they all align. Figure 5 is an example. The basic family tree can be embellished by adding titles, extra text and drawings using the program's facilities, or scanned photographs, maps and documents can be imported and added. The Mac allows you to copy items easily from one document and paste them into another via the Clipboard, even if they are created with different programs. You can only move one item at a time via the clipboard though, and if you want to use a drawing, photo or piece of text frequently, you can store it in the scrap-book file. You can copy and paste several images into the scrapbook at a time before returning to your chart to paste them in. You can keep some images stored permanently in the scrapbook, where they will always be available for adding to documents, useful if you want to create a logo and add it to your letters and documents for instance.

Communications

This is the final program included in most of the integrated packages, and unless you buy a modem, it will be of no use to you. Attaching a modem and using this program will give you a simple means of connecting your computer to another computer, a bulletin board, or to transfer files to another computer via a standard telephone line. If you want access to the World Wide Web and the Internet, you will probably want to connect to an on-line service like Compuserve. Your on-line service provider will often provide you with a suite of programs which are tailored to suit their facilities, making Email and Internet access much simpler.

It can be seen from this chapter that you could manage to store and present all your family history information by using one of the integrated packages or the equivalent stand alone packages (a rather more expensive option). There is a booklet available on using the spreadsheet for genealogy, "Spreadsheet Family Trees" by G. Lawton and there have been several interesting articles in past editions of "Family Tree" magazine's computer section, on using spreadsheets, databases and word processing programs in genealogy.

Having committed yourself to using a computer though, it would really make more sense to obtain a specialist Genealogy program, designed to give the facilities you need as a family historian. Then your other programs can be used in a supporting role. Specially written genealogy databases vary a great deal in both cost and content, so the next two chapters will describe most of what is available for the Macintosh.

Chapter 3 : Shareware genealogy programs

Because PC's are much more common than Macs, PC owners have been well catered for with a wide range of low cost, shareware genealogical titles, from authors in Britain as well as the USA. You may have heard of programs such as Pedigree, Cumberland Tree or Brother's Keeper which have helped to make family history an easier and more rewarding pastime for many people. Mac genealogy programs are thin on the ground, with only a limited range of both shareware and commercial programs to choose from. The good side of this is that you can take time to look at all of them before deciding.

When I started, I investigated the UK shareware market first, to see just what was available, and my findings are listed in this chapter. I had decided to try a little family research using a cheap shareware program before I decided if it was for me, but by the time I had tried them all out, I was hooked and bought a full featured commercial program to organise my new hobby.

What is Shareware?

Shareware is software that is available on a try before you buy basis, usually written by enthusiasts who charge very little for the use of their programs. You buy a disc containing a copy of the program, try it out at home on your own computer for a reasonable time, say 30 days, then if you like it you send the author a cheque; if you don't, you stop using the program.

Before registration, some software will limit the number of entries that can be made into the data files, others rely purely upon your honesty to collect their fees, if you continue to use the program you are morally, if not legally, obliged to pay the fee. However payment of the fee often brings enhanced versions and more comprehensive user manuals to reward your integrity, as well as notification of further updates.

The shareware mentioned in this article was supplied by a specialist supplier. Names of shareware suppliers may be found in the small ads that appear at the back of the various Macintosh computer magazines, or you can buy them direct from the author concerned.

The cost of acquiring all the programs listed here came to just a few pounds, excellent value when you consider that you can evaluate the programs fully to see which best meets your needs. Remember though that the money you pay to the shareware supplier is not the shareware fee due to the author, but only the cost of the disk and copying the program for you.

GEDCOM data transfer standard

If you have read a little about genealogical computing, you may have come across this acronym and wondered just what it was. Well, it is an important part of any good genealogical program, being the means of moving all your family's information from one program to another. It is a file transfer standard developed by the LDS Church to work with their family history programs and adopted by other software writers. Because of the variations between programs, GEDCOM transfers are not always as smooth as you might think, see David Hawgood's booklet "GEDCOM Data Transfer

(Moving your Family Tree)". Use a program without it, and you will be faced with re-typing everything from scratch if you want to upgrade programs, unfortunately it is not a standard supported by many of the shareware programs!

Hypercard Stack Programs

Macintosh computers used to come supplied with a program called Hypercard™, this is actually a simple to use programming system in which standard routines can be assembled and then used to perform all sorts of linked functions. This has been used by many enthusiasts to create their own custom programs for genealogy, with widely varied results. Users often have very different views as to what and how they want the program to perform, so the emphasis on a program's functions varies from one author to another. Your priority may be to hold and sort thousands of entries under just one category, whilst the next person may want only a couple of hundred entries, with the priority on presenting the information as neat family trees, so you need to decide just what you want from a program.

The first few programs are Hypercard stacks (the stack is the instructions which form the application) and need this commercial program installed in the computer to work. Some stacks are designed to enable customising by the user, which is alright as long as you are prepared to learn Hypercard programming, otherwise you will have to accept them as they come.

The Hypercard stack programs tend to be less sophisticated and slower than many of the other programs, and most were written quite a long time ago. If you only want a simple program or an introduction to family history for your children, then they may suffice, but I find them frustratingly pedestrian.

Family Tree 1.0 : This has all the normal database functions and it will in addition store digitised photographs and act as a family contact manager, looking after addresses, birthday lists, linking to a word-processor to write letters and even phoning family members for you!

Shareware fee $5.
Author : Jim Palms. PO Box 70218, Belleview, WA98007, USA.

Genealogy Data Base 1.1 : Also found listed as Genealogy Stack. Another simple but reasonably well laid out database program.

Shareware fee $5
Author : Kevin Mennitt, 208 Baker Avenue, Westfield, NJ 07090, USA

Genealogy Explorer : I came across a demo version of this program which was a browse only version, with data on English Monarchs. It will not produce charts or pedigrees. See Genealogical Computing July 1993 p.29.

Shareware fee $30
Publisher : Food for Thought Software, 9235 Fern Ln., Des Plaines,

IL 60016, USA.

Genealogy Research Helper 1.0 : Also found listed as GENE 1.0. This is the largest and to my mind, the best of the Hypercard stacks that I have tried. It has a much more comprehensive range of well presented cards than the others. The data is stored on these from a wide range of sources such as census returns, probate and court information etc. It can produce simple charts and can also record the LDS Church information if required. Various additions are promised by the author, but I don't know if they were ever implemented, worth looking at if you have Hypercard.

Shareware fee $10.
Author : David Brewer, 827 East 930 North, Pleasant Grove, Utah 84062, USA.

Hyper Tree 1.2 : A simple interactive database with a rather peculiar card layout and design but it is Freeware!

Author : Joe Crnich
Available from MacPow's shareware library.

Our Family Tree 1.3 : Another simple relational card database, but with rather better laid out cards, it could be used as a good introduction to family history for younger members of the family. Requires the True Type™ font Goudy Mediaeval for the trees it prints.

Shareware fee $10
Author : Timmy G. Bremer, 19 Town Garden Drive, Appart.4, Liverpool, New York 13088, USA

Two other Hypercard programs were mentioned in Macworld's genealogy program review in the June 1995 edition : **Branches** and **Genealogy 2.1**, but I haven't come across either of these in the UK to evaluate them.

The previous programmes all required Hypercard which if you don't already own it, is a fairly expensive commercial program, but they may work with Hypercard Player™. This is a cut down version of the program, which will certainly enable you to have a good look at stacks. Stacks may need converting before they can be operated with Hypercard Player. This player program, as far as I know is not a Shareware program, but it was given away on the cover disc of the August 94 edition of Macworld, if you can get a back copy. The Hypercard offerings are often clever, some are well designed, but in my opinion, they are not really suitable for any serious genealogy.

Programs not requiring Hypercard

The following are stand alone programs not requiring any other commercial programs to enable them to run. I particularly like Heritage 2.6 and Gene 4.1, they both use a name list as the starting screen, making browsing and navigation through the data easy.

With Gene 4.1 you can start typing a name and it will automatically match what you type to the list of entries, an automatic sort function which saves much time when you have hundreds of names to scroll through.

Family Events 1.5 : A well featured, slightly unusual program which was reviewed in the June 1995 edition of Macworld. The reviewer was obviously impressed, but I haven't found a copy available from a UK source. It works like a cardboard box, into which you feed your scraps of information from each family event or research document. It then constructs your family tree from the data, it also supports GEDCOM file transfer.

Shareware fee $35
Publisher : Magreeable Software, 5925 Magnolia Lane, Plymouth, MN 55442-1573, USA

GENE 4.1 : I judge this to be the best of the limited range of genealogical shareware available for the Mac, by this I don't mean that it is the bet of a "bad lot", but that it stands head and shoulders over the others.

Gene is a quick and easy to learn, fast, professional, genealogy database program, written by Diana and David Eppstein. It stores genealogical information on various cards representing people, places, pictures, and events etc. The number of card types has now been increased to eleven, and the individual's card rather than a family card is the key to browsing easily through all the information stored on other cards.

(See next page)

The person card or window, as shown in Figure 6, is split into three fields: the identity field containing name, birth and parent details; the linked field which lists the links to other cards containing details of marriages, births, deaths, events, photographs, documents etc., and the third field is a notes field. A report summary of the number and type of cards can be displayed, and each of the different card types and their contents can be listed too.

The program can store all your family data plus extensive notes, and it is fast, even on low end Macs like the Classic. One of it's strongest features is the extensive use of linking, you can simply browse the database by clicking on names in cards and trees or on photographs. Simply clicking on a name or photograph will instantly bring up that persons record card, with it's associated links to data stored on other cards.

Gene's straightforward user interface has drawn praise from other people too: "The look of this prodigiously likeable little shareware item should be the envy of designers of more expensive software" [David Pogue, Macworld magazine, June 1995, p. 147].

Although Gene is easy to use, it is not a simple program, and is capable of handling very complicated databases with thousands of names, multiple marriages and divorces, adoptions, illegitimate children, intermarriage between relatives, notes and references.

A very good Hypertext user guide comes with the program, complete with an associated Hypertext reading program, it is very clear and comprehensive and although access to help is not available from within the program (hopefully that will come later),

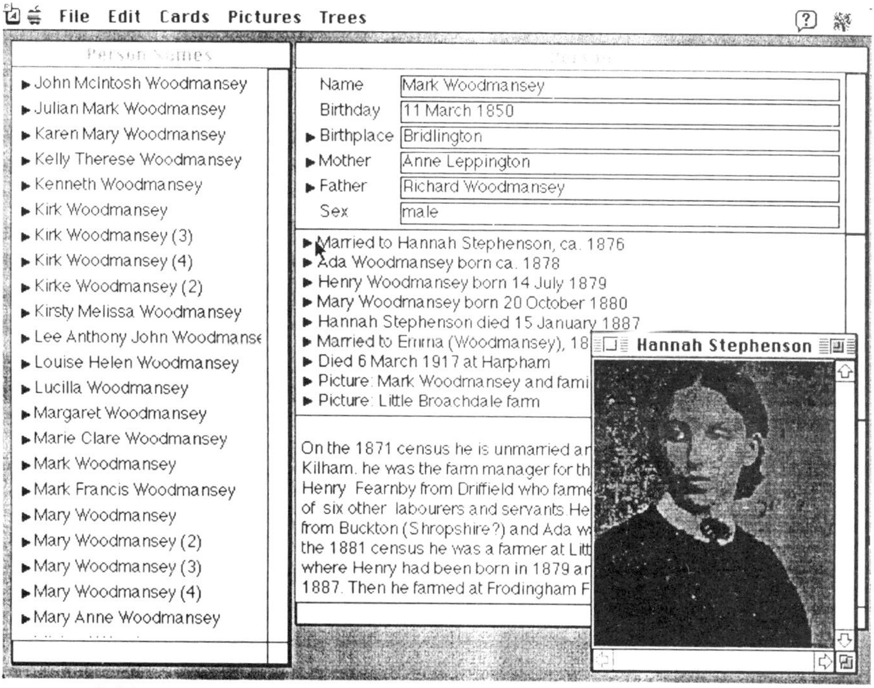

Figure 6. Initially navigating a GENE database from the name index connects you to the persons card, which has direct links to other directly related person cards as well as those containing photographs. The Person card is split into three fields : personal information : links to other connected event or person cards : notes field.

with System 7.0 you can leave it running in the background to consult when necessary anyway. There is also a Simpletext version included in the folder, which is slower to use, but is suitable for printing out as a user manual.

One of the main failings of the original version of this program was it's failure to support GEDCOM import and export of data, leaving you with the daunting process of re-typing all your data if you wanted to change programs, and making it impossible to exchange data easily with other researchers. This deficiency has now been fixed and I tested it by transferring some data to Reunion, the program I normally use. GEDCOM transfer is not quite always as straightforward as you might expect from a "Transfer Standard", it does seem to suffer from variations in the way different programs use and store information. Reunion accepted the exported file happily, but was not happy with the extensive research notes on some cards, and part of these were posted to Reunion's custom fields, leaving a bit of cutting and pasting before the information was all ship-shape again. It was easily spotted though, and it is easy to open the original GEDCOM file with a word-processor to see what the information should read like. Anyhow it took very little sorting out, and a test file of about eighty persons was up and running in the time it would have taken me to type only a handful of cards from scratch. The user guide notes a GEDCOM problem that may be encountered in transferring marriages without date and place, because of the different ways programs deal with this information. When importing information into Gene, any information it doesn't know what to do with, is put into the notes field.

The other major improvement in the new version is it's ability to store photographs of people places, documents etc., in fact anything that can be scanned and stored in PICT format. It is not yet able to place these on the family trees (perhaps this might be in the next version too!) however you are able to define button areas on the photographs and link these back to other cards - see Figure 7. This is a super feature for those large family photographs, where a button can be created for each person, linking their image to their person cards and the background linked to a place card perhaps. This feature is a luxurious touch that would be a useful addition to some of the commercial programs.

As well as GEDCOM and picture handling added to this latest version of the program, many other minor changes and additions have taken place, removing most of the petty annoyances that make using many shareware programs seem like a second class option. There is a preferences dialogue box which enables you to set the default settings on start-up exactly how you want them. You can define the fonts, sizes, date formats and many other items which before, had to be altered every time you used the program, and the cursor pointer now helpfully changes to a hand, when it is over an active link button. These are the little refinements missing from so many shareware programs, that make using this program a pleasure.

The tree drawing facility has been extended in the latest edition too. You can now view and print four types of chart: Ancestor Grid, Relations, Descendants or Ancestors, in a choice of three different styles: Name only, Terse or Verbose. This facility enables you to draw and print clear informative trees, with the added bonus that every name on the displayed tree on the screen is also a link button back to that persons details card. This gives you another useful way to browse the information stored in the database, because you can jump from branch to branch without having to navigate through every linked person. Again, this is a feature not present on some commercial programs. You cannot yet edit these charts and add notes or photographs, but that may yet come.

What would you get if you paid many times as much as Gene 4.1's modest shareware fee, and bought a full commercial program? Well, you may be able to re-arrange the boxes and add photographs to the printouts of trees, and you could probably do more sophisticated filter searches, and get reports printed, but if these are not high priorities, then Gene will now do all the basics. It displays and prints good clear charts, and will do simple name searches, which is probably all you would require to start, and then it adds a few nice luxury touches too.

Gene 4.1 is a value packed, fast and professional program with many more features

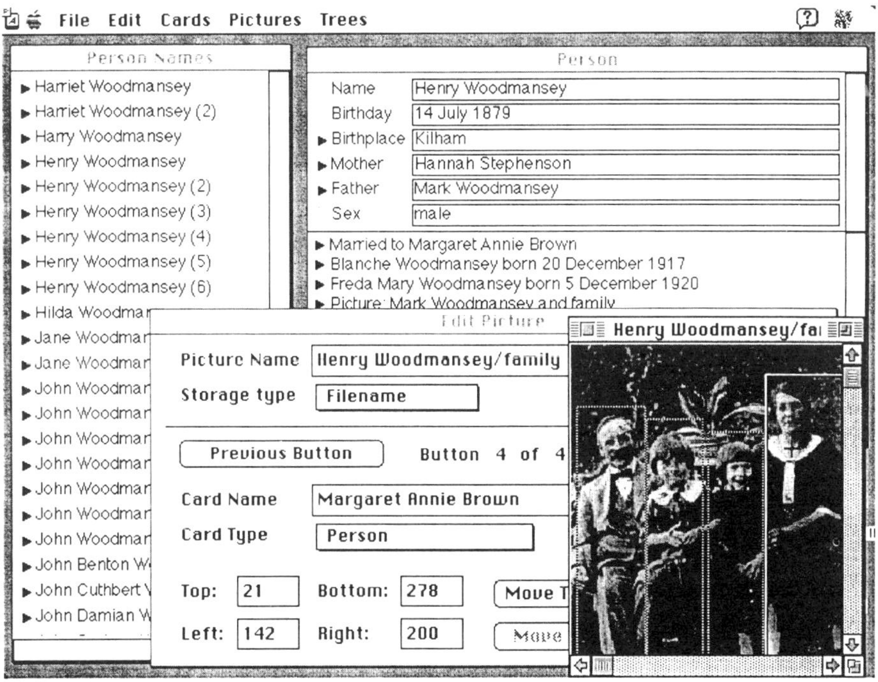

Figure 7. A nice feature with GENE is that link buttons may be set on different parts of photographs to connect them with the correct Person card, allowing you to navigate from person to person in a family photo, even if they are only distantly related.

than you would expect for it's modest $15 fee. If you want a really useful, budget priced family history program for Macintosh, this is it, and by supporting the authors and giving them feedback it should continue to improve, becoming a benchmark program on the Mac.

Shareware Fee $15
David and Dianna Eppstein, 8 Owen Ct., Irvine, CA 92715, USA
email: eppstein@ics.uci.edu
Send shareware fee $15 plus $5 p&p or download it from the authors' web page :
http://www.ics.uci.edu/~eppstein/gene/

You can get a copy of GENE 4.1 in the UK from :
S&N Genealogy Supplies, 5 Polden Close, Farnborough, Hampshire,
GU14 9H; phone 01252 510486
or from the author of this book:
David Tippey, Victoria Lodge, Kirkby Malham nr Skipton, North Yorkshire, BD23 4BS; phone 01729 830547
Send £4 incl. P&P for program on HD disk.

Genealogy Pro : This is an another rather different program, this time from Australia. It is chart orientated, and uses the family tree as the main interface to your information. Unfortunately the demo version I received from a shareware supplier had screen scrolling problems and I was not able to evaluate it.

Heritage 2.1 : Very easy data entry, with no limit on the number of people, marriages or children per person. Can display and store digitised photographs and large biographical files, linked to the person's name. It is one of the few shareware programs that supports GEDCOM import and export. It can display family group sheets, although these are not particularly well laid out, but it doesn't produce trees at present. When a name is highlighted from the people list, then various information can be called up via the menu bar.

This is a program which is rapidly evolving, with many additions promised. Currently it is a very good "front end" of a program, the output side of which now needs developing, but it promises to be a very useful program in the future. The unregistered version is limited to 40 entries and requires System 7.0.

Shareware fee $15
Publisher : TAG Software, 14049, 232 Ave SE, Issaquah, WA 98007, USA

MacRoots 7.0.1 : A fairly sophisticated Genealogical program which is able to create and edit a family database, view relationships to other members and view and print a complete range of charts. It is not as quick to use as some, especially when you first start using it. It was reviewed in Family Tree Computer magazine Nov 1992 p.29 and MacRoots II a commercial version was reviewed in Genealogical Computing July 1993.

Shareware fee $45.
Publisher : Itasca Softworks, Box 427, Bagley, MN 56621, USA

Suppliers of shareware and demonstration programs

It is sometimes also possible to get trial or demo versions of commercial programs from shareware suppliers. These demos like some of the shareware versions only accept a limited number of entries and often have some functions disabled.

The shareware and demo versions of a number of commercial programs are available from various shareware distributors advertising in Mac computer magazines, as well as from the authors, if you can't find a supplier try :-

Stormont Software, 9 Reaville Park, Dundonald, Belfast, BT16 0AR

MacPow, 96 John Street, Brierly Hill, West Midlands, DY5 1HF

who both produce a shareware catalogue on disk, or

S&N Genealogy Supplies, 5 Polden Close, Farnborough, Hampshire, GU14 9HN. Phone/fax 01252 378054.

or the author of this book, David Tippey, Victoria Lodge, Kirkby Malham, Skipton, North Yorkshire BD23 4BS; phone 01729 830547.

Chapter 4 : Commercial genealogy programs

Commercial genealogy programs cost more than shareware, but on the whole are more fully featured and have some kind of user support from the publisher. Only four commercial genealogy programs are readily available to Macintosh users in the UK: Family Roots, Personal Ancestral File (PAF), ProGen and Reunion.

Family Heritage File 3.3
Reviewed in Macworld June 1995, and not as far as I know, supplied by anyone in the UK. It contains many good features let down by the interface, it is not one program, but 32 applications in one folder. David Pogue says of it,"if Family Heritage File were a true Macintosh program, it may be tolerable"

Costs $149, Published by StarCom Microsystems, USA. tel. 801 225 1480

Family Roots 3.7
The program is basically in three parts, data storing, tree making and printing, sorting and indexing. It will print 4-5 generation pedigrees and also blank stationery charts and LDS family sheets. The program supports GEDCOM data transfer. Although it has plenty of features, the interface is not your usual Mac user-friendly screen. A trial version which will accept 30 entries and only works from a floppy disc is available from shareware houses, but it has no Quit and entails restarting the computer to exit the program! See the review in Macworld June 1995, where David Pogue described it as "a respectable genealogy program trapped inside a mess of an interface" , other reviews have appeared in Family Tree Computer Magazine, November 1992 and Genealogical Computing, September 1984 and March 1987.

Costs £99
Distributed by TRACS, 94 Coombe Lane, Bristol, BS9 2AP; phone 01179 686768, contact Tony Reese.
Published by Quinsept, USA
Trial version from MacPow

MacRoots II: A fairly sophisticated, but simple to use genealogical program which is able to create and edit a family database, view relationships to other members and view and print a complete range of charts and supports GEDCOM. It is not as quick to use as some, especially when you first start using it. The shareware version was reviewed in Family Tree Computer magazine Nov 1992 p.29 and MacRoots II was reviewed in Genealogical Computing July 1993 and Macworld June 1995 where David Pogue says " MacRoots just doesn't go far enough". MacRoots II 2.0 was issued in August 1995, and has been reviewed favourably by Larry Naukam in Genealogical Computing Jan/Mar 1996 (p36). MacRoots II requires a minimum of a Mac Plus and a hard disk drive. 2 megabytes of memory is preferable. A free demo is available.

Cost $99 including overseas postage. Telephone orders: (601) 255-8677; Fax orders: (601) 255-7086. Postal orders: Itasca Softworks, 3 Leisure Time Drive, Diamondhead, MS 39535, USA.

Personal Ancestral File 2.1 for Macintosh

Published by the LDS church, Personal Ancestral File has been available for a long time and is starting to show it's age. An updated version has long been promised, but as yet still failed to materialise, however it is workman-like and has satisfied the needs of many researchers, although the Mac version does not have all the features of the PC one. It has been reviewed many times, including one in "Computers in Genealogy" in June 1993, when Brian Randell wrote an article comparing version 3.8 of Reunion with Personal Ancestral File. There are not many choices in family history programs for Macintosh and PAF has always been a popular, budget choice "entry level" program to computer genealogy.

The presentation of what is basically a shareware priced family history package is very good. The disks come with pre-printed labels for your working copies, a short quick reference guide book and that great luxury, a well presented, spiral bound user guide, which lays flat on the table and doesn't change page as soon as you look back at the monitor.

The package is actually a collection of three programs: the Family Records program, the main genealogical database, which uses as it's interface, a family card (Figure 8) similar to programs like Reunion; the Research Data Filer program, a pre-formatted database used for storing and sorting information on people and events which are possibly related to your research; and PAFCOM , a very basic communications program, which will allow you to exchange GEDCOM files via a modem.

When you read the instructions for installing and using the programs, they have a somewhat dated feel, which will make owners of the Mac Plus feel totally at home. Here we were talking about computers with RAM the size of a pocket handkerchief, two disk drives if you were lucky and Macintosh operating System 3.2!! Hard drives were obviously a rarity in 1988/9 and are dismissed in four lines, with no mention of warning you not to put a copy of System 3.2 (included on the self-booting program disk) onto the hard disk of a machine already containing a System on the hard disk.

I know that some people are still happily using such machines, which have probably given 8-10 years of reliable service, but High Street shops are now selling multi media machines with 8Mb of Ram, 500Mb Hard disks and quad speed CD ROMs, almost as standard. The most likely buys on the second-hand market are LC's and higher which have at least 2Mb of RAM and a 40Mb hard disk. Updated instructions taking account of some of these changes, even a loose sheet, would certainly not have gone amiss, even if the program itself hadn't changed.

PAF is a very "Worthy" data base, but is poor at the presentation of all your family data. Printouts from this program will not be much help in stimulating the interest of aunt Nelly in your researches, they look like they have just come from a 1970's government report.

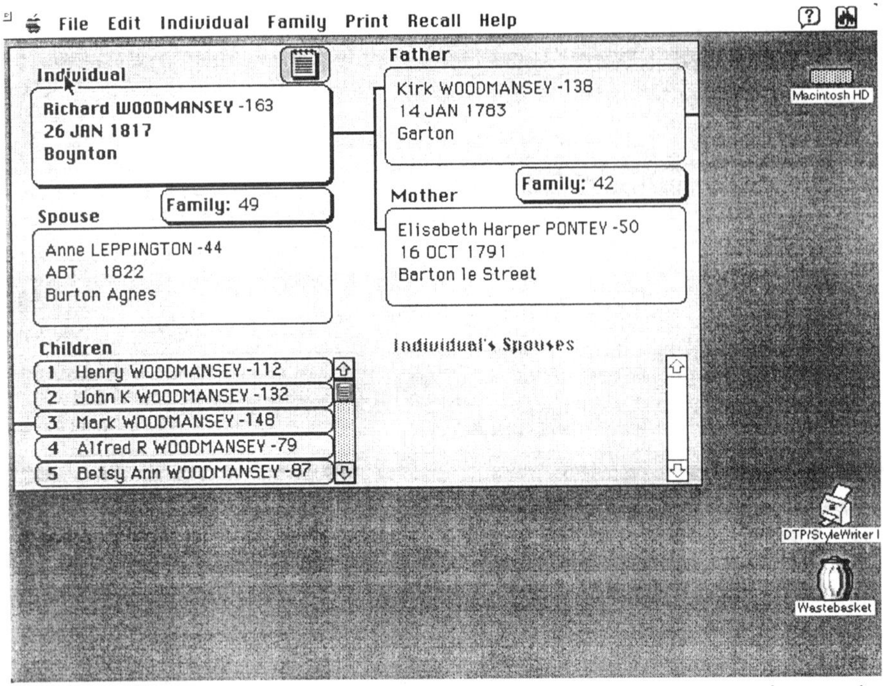

Figure 8 The main screen of PAF is a family card, which allows you to navigate to the individuals. Unfortunately you cannot re-size this window to fit your monitor, although you can change it's colour!

PC owners have had the many shortfalls in PAF compensated for by a plethora of shareware utilities and add-ons, which draw charts, create book style reports etc. The Mac is not so well served, so users are stuck with the un-enhanced database facilities offered by PAF back in 1988.

Having said that, Family Records is an able genealogical database, and the Research Data Filer program is useful too, but sooner or later most family historians will want facilities which allow for the production of more interesting and professional looking charts and reports, allow complex searches, store and use photographs and all the other facilities which make computer genealogy less like the traditional card index.

The maximum field lengths of only 16 characters can be a problem, leading to strange, truncated entries, particularly for place names, which regularly contain many more characters than this (see Figure 9). If you try and download IGI information straight into PAF from Family Search (see next chapter), truncation of long fields can be a problem too. For example, a GEDCOM file when read with a word processor program contained the address " *Bethel Chapel North Street Bridge Street New Connexion, Kingston Upon Hull, Yorkshire, England*", but transferred to PAF this appeared as "*Bethel Chapel No, Kingston Upon Hu, Yorkshire, England*". The entry had been chopped down to sixteen characters between each comma to fit the field, but what is more worrying is the total absence of the missing data from the unused data listing prepared by PAF.

If a budget priced, Macintosh genealogical database is what you want, then the aging PAF might, despite minor annoyances still fit the bill, although I would give the excellent shareware program Gene 4.1 a good hard look first, before parting with my money.

Costs £27.90 (check before ordering; version 2.31 may be available).
Published by: The Church of Jesus Christ of Latter-day Saints. UK Distribution Centre: 399 Garretts Green Lane, Birmingham, B33 OV4. Phone 0121 784 9555.

PAF Shareware Add-ons: I found the following four programs available on Compuserve, and they may be of interest to anyone who is already running PAF. The entries here are copied straight from the Compuserve ROOTS genealogical directory. You can get someone with a modem to download them for you, or as I have not come across a UK supplier I (David Tippey) will supply them - see end of Chapter 3 for address.

AF2MP.SIT : This Macintosh utility AF2MacPAF will take a GEDCOM file that was created by the LDS "Ancestral File" program and "clean" it up by translating the little inconsistencies where Mac PAF and Ancestral File disagree on what a GEDCOM file ought to look like.

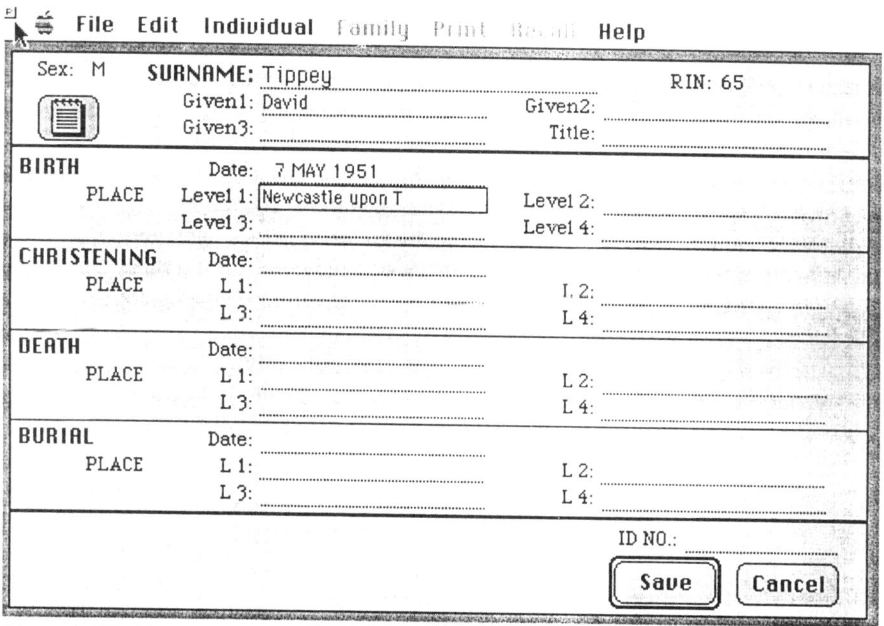

Figure 9 Clicking on a person's name on the family card brings up the individual's detail card. Unfortunately the field lengths are rather short resulting in the truncation of some information.

MPRU12.SIT : MacPAF Report Utility (MPRU) provides a number of lists & reports to be generated from genealogical databases created by the Macintosh Personal Ancestral File system. MPRU 1.2 adds data extracts, reduces memory requirements & fixes many minor defects. Reports & lists include: person/place name frequencies, individual, family, relational table extracts, root family, note summary, & soundex code lists and ahnentafel and cascading descendant charts. This version is for all Macs. Shareware by Joe Oglesby.

MACPAF.SEA : MacPAF Utility is an add-on to the LDS program PAF/Family Records. The utility can create many additional reports and provides export services as well, so data can be charted into a spreadsheet for example. Additionally, MacPAF Utility allows you to maintain a photo repository so you can have photos linked to your RIN and MRIN records. Version 1.1 introduces an improved user interface as well as a few minor enhancements.
Shareware by Chris Miksanek.

RDF2GE.SIT : RDF-to-GEDCOM for the Macintosh-
This Mac program will convert GEDCOM files to PAF Research Data Filer (RDF) files and PAF's RDF files to GEDCOM. This makes it convenient to use the powerful sort and focus routines in RDF and be able to port records back and forth to Family Records. On-line help included.
Shareware by Blake A. Rosenvall.

ProGen 1.2
This British program won it's author "Young Software Designer of the Year" in 1991. It is simple to use and offers unlimited entry of Personal Records and Individual Events, plus unlimited user definable event types. The main interface screen has an excellent help bar which will assist your learning it's operation, but it's graphic design is a little quirky. It has good reporting and search facilities and is GEDCOM compatible. This version has an improved interface, will produce photo drop-line trees and user definable reports. Version1.1 for the Mac had some problems, but the new updated version, hopefully fully de-bugged is now available.

Costs £69.95
Published by : Gensoft, 70 Nelson Road, Ipswich IP4 4DT; phone 01473 724674.

Reunion 4

Unlike PAF, a lot of changes have taken place since version 3.8 of Reunion was compared with Personal Ancestral File by Brian Randell, in the review previously referred to. Reunion is a well featured, flexible genealogical database, whose authors are constantly trying to upgrade with new additional innovations.

Originally, Reunion was a clever implementation of the Hypercard application development utility that originally came bundled with the early Macintosh computers. The program was so good, compared to many plodding, shareware Hypercard genealogy offerings however, that it was possible to overlook the fact that it was a Hypercard program at all. Leister Productions have re-written the software in Version 4 to do away with Hypercard and it now carries out what used to be slow functions, like list building for example, at 3 or 4 times the speed of the earlier versions. This means that the program runs at a respectable speed even on entry level Macs. Nevertheless like most major program updates it now also requires more RAM to operate, your computer will need at least 4 Mb, as well as running System 7 or newer, and if you want to update to version 4 from an earlier version, you will need to do it by using a GEDCOM file, because the two programs operate so differently.

Reunion will allow you to have up to 30,000 individuals in one family file, with up to 20 children per couple, and 26 spouses per individual which should cover the needs of most people except for dog breeders apparently (yes there are other uses for genealogy programs besides keeping track of aunt Nelly). The program was reviewed

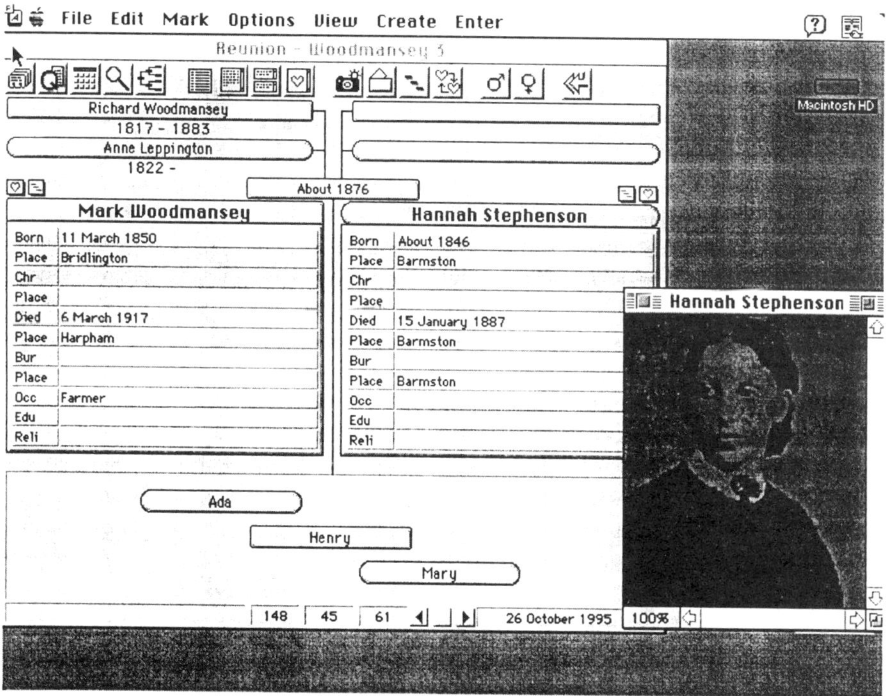

Figure 10 The main screen of REUNION displays one family group, with direct links to individual's data, notes (see Fig 11) and photographs.

in Macworld June 1995, where David Pogue says " Reunion isn't just an outstanding genealogy program, it's an outstanding program, *period*." It was also featured in MacUser, 13th October 1995, where Keith Brindley says "British genealogists should rejoice, for there's really nothing else quite like it."

Data entry is straightforward, and despite the program's flexibility, the program is relatively simple to use and comes with a very clear and comprehensive manual. Scanned photographs and documents, stored in PICT format, are easily linked to the family cards, and up to 999 reference notes per family can now be associated to the card too.

An interesting addition is the date interpretation function, which allows you to enter dates in the same way as they would be spoken, for example you could type in "7 years after birth" and the program will automatically create the date in your standard date format, selected from one of the 16 styles available.

Version 4 now sports a family card (Figures 10 and 11) re-designed for the larger colour monitors, which can be re-sized to fit the screen, with the button bar across the top or on either side. This screen is your main way of navigating from family to family, however you also can navigate from the "overview" window (Figure 12), which is like a small pedigree chart giving you a larger picture of your files.

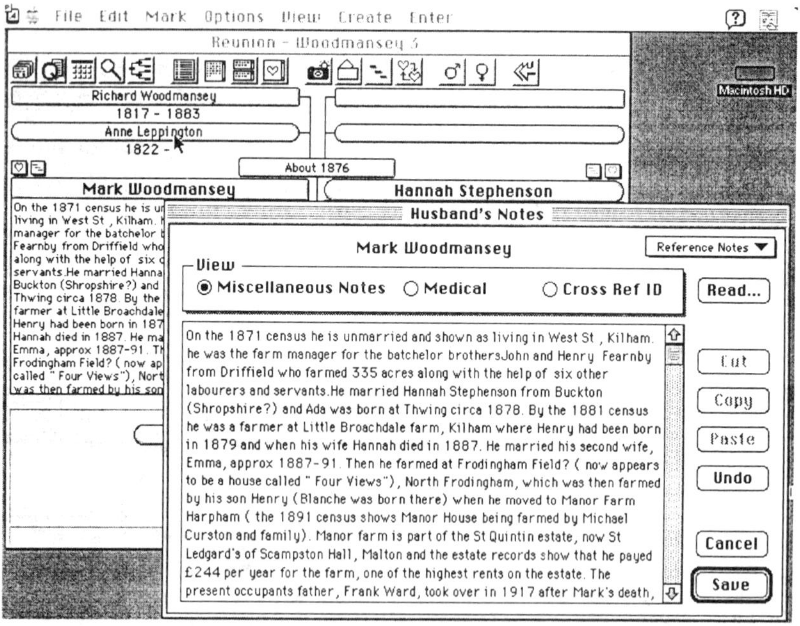

Figure 11 You can keep extensive notes for each individual with cross reference ID's and notes for your sources.

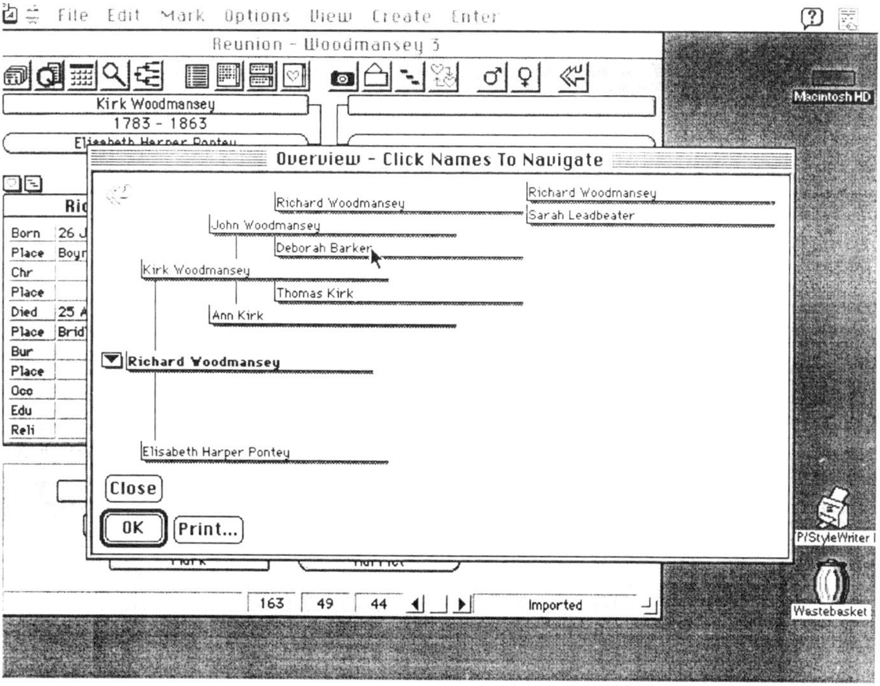

Figure 12 REUNION allows you to navigate using a family chart too, allowing you to sidestep to a cousins line for instance without having to work back down the line to the progenitor and then forwards again.

Indexing has been improved by allowing the contents of two additional fields of your choice (see Figure 13); by listing their parents for example, you could make it much easier to sort out similarly named ancestors.

The Automark search facility has been made more powerful and offers more choices in search conditions, up to two conditions at once with the option of using AND or OR. You can list and view the sorted cards before marking and it will work out your relationship to an ancestor for up to 255 generations!

Seven different report types are now available including two book style ones: Ahnentafel, ancestor reports and the Register report, which is a more narrative version of the Family History descendant report and an index listing of all persons in the data base with the option of listing two additional personal facts. There are several formatting options with all the reports so that you can choose what data is included.

All reports are automatically opened through your own word processor, and the program neatly formats page numbers, breaks, tabs, superscript reference notes etc. automatically. The big advantage of using your WP, is that you have complete final control of the finished document. It is created on your WP program, so you do not have to accept standard report formats, and fonts, if you don't like them, then the look of your documents is only limited by your WP's. facilities.

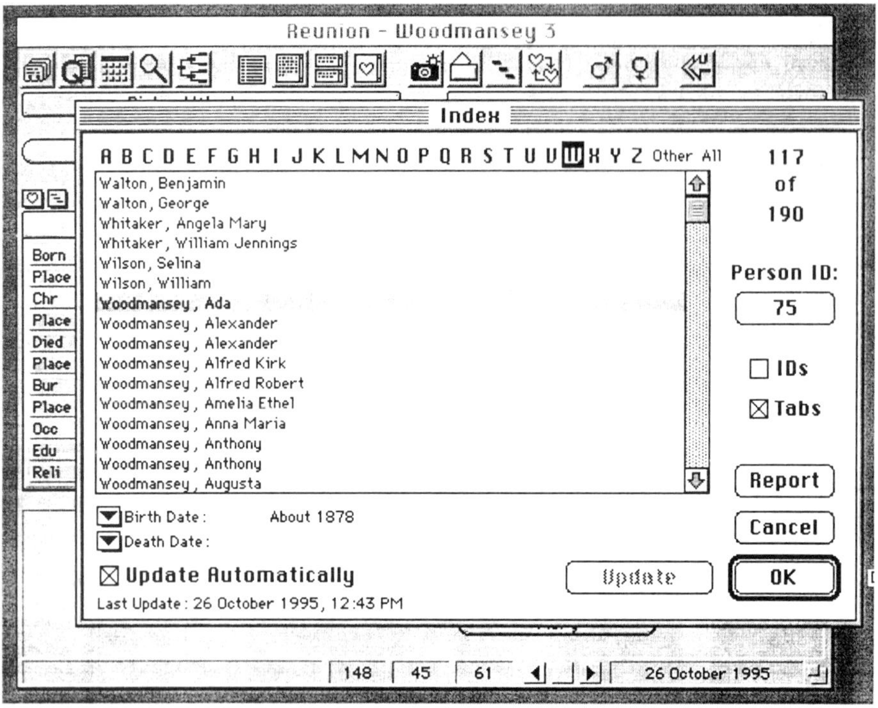

Figure 13 Like many other programs, REUNION keeps a master index of all names in the database, but it allows you to search by name plus two other selected pieces of information such as birth date or place too. The index can be printed as a report, including this additional information

Four or five generation cascading pedigree charts can be printed, which are cross referenced with continuation numbers and allow up to 34 generations. Family group sheets and Person sheets can now be created, in normal and questionnaire form, which shows which facts are unknown, and formatted blank forms can be printed too.

Charts like Figure 14 are created using the associated program SuperChart, which is launched automatically when one of it's functions is selected. It will create up to a 99 generation descendant chart or 35 generation pedigree chart in three styles: Left to Right, Top to Bottom and Waterfall.

Chart boxes can be colour coded, and can be dragged around and the program will automatically re-draw the links, although you may end up with crossed links if you are not careful.

Charts can be printed up to 455 inches square, and to help you re-arrange the boxes so that they do not fall on page breaks, these are shown on the on-screen charts; see Figure 15. You can zoom out to get an overview of an entire multi-sheet chart, re-arrange the boxes, then zoom back in for a final adjustments. However you will need a Mac with a fast processor if you want to work with large charts.

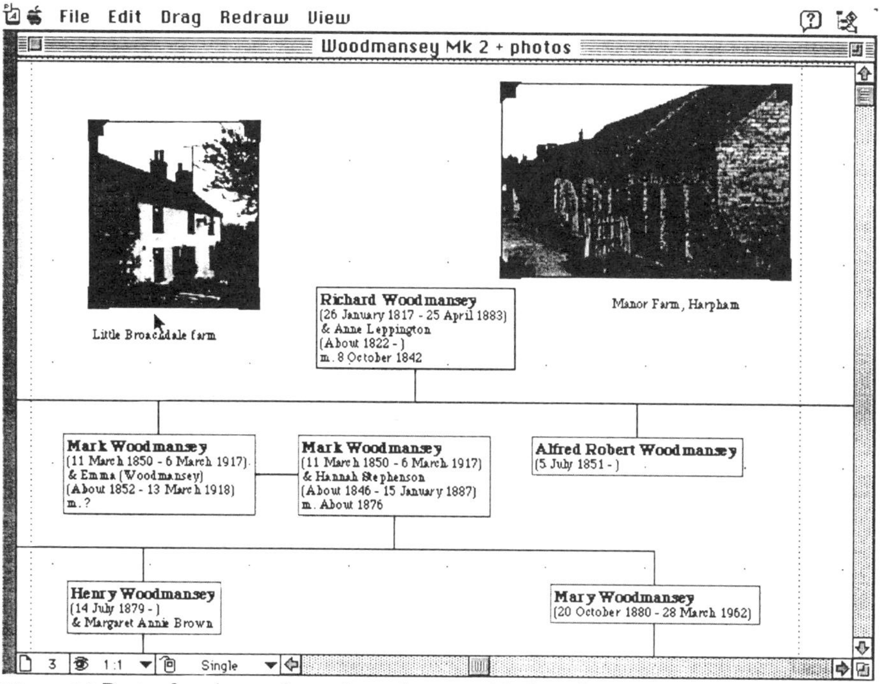

Figure 14 Part of a descendant chart drawn with Reunion's tree drawing program Superchart. Charts can be drawn in several styles and can include pictures and additional text.

Extra labelling is easily added to the charts and photographs can be included and re-sized too. However the implementation of this is not quite as smooth as it might be, because the Mac's Clipboard file has to be used to copy the photographs to the charts, requiring swapping backward and forward between the two programs. Direct access from SuperChart would be a big improvement, so would the ability to store short video clips, now that multi-media computers are becoming more available. The other problem I found was that the chart's box formats (short or tall) are selected whilst in Reunion and cannot be changed from within SuperChart, which is a nuisance if it needs changing so that the chart will just fit on a certain number of pages for instance.

You can easily exchange GEDCOM files with other researchers, and Reunion files can be read and manipulated by both the Macintosh and the PC versions of the program, no matter which version created them. In the past I have sent WP files of various reports created by Reunion to computer owners who didn't have a GEDCOM compatible program. Leister have now made available via the Internet a downloadable "Reunion Player" program, which will open a "Transfer File" created by Reunion. Available in Mac and Windows formats it is a browse only program which allows them to look through the data, including notes and references, use the index and display the pedigree overviews, but not create proper charts.

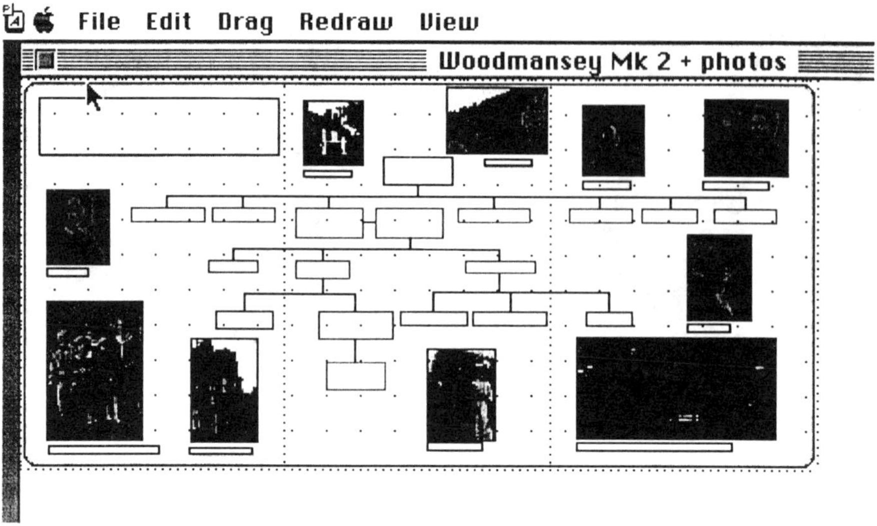

Figure 15 Overview of a multisheet chart with pictures, allows you to make sure that an individuals information is not split between sheets. You can create massive charts and include pictures etc. too, but your machine might appear to be "running through treacle", so it is best to split charts up into manageable sections rather than try to create a "global" one.

Reunion 4 is an excellent, easy to use, all round program, and although you can always think of some extras you would like included, it is already better featured than other Mac programs I have tried. Leister already have plans for version 5, due in 1996, with extra features promised, such as timelines and a system for finding and removing duplicates. It is a program which is a pleasure to use, very flexible and comprehensive, with charts and reports that are going to make your family research really create an impression. If you are using an earlier version of Reunion and have sufficient memory to run version 4, then I would seriously consider upgrading, I don't think you would be disappointed.

Costs £85. A demonstration version is available at £3.
Published by : Leister Productions, USA
Available from :-
S&N Genealogy Supplies, 5 Polden Close, Farnborough, Hampshire,
GU14 9H; phone/fax 01252 378054.

Chapter 5:
Computer readable research data: availability and use

Some records are becoming available in computer readable forms now, as well as the printed or microfiche/film ones you may be used to. This is the obvious direction for record keeping to go, how I wish that I could search the Indexes of St Catherine's House for all the Births, Deaths and Marriages of the Tippey's using a computer terminal. I would be finished in an hour, and as it is, I have spent days winding reels of microfilm by hand and haven't yet worked my way through half of the births 1837-1900! At present the machine readable records available for the UK are not very extensive, but a vast range of American Census and other Indexes and some Australian Record indexes are available in CD ROM form. Unfortunately people still seem rather paranoid about data held on computers, and the most recent major project, the 1881 Census Index, although prepared on computer is only being made available on microfiche! So we are doomed to search through hundreds of fiche for the entire country, to pick up any possible stray entries for our family research, I despair!

However there is some useful data available for UK genealogists to work with on their own computers, and a useful starting point is to find your nearest Mormon Family History Centre.

LDS Church Family History Centres : These are Branch Libraries of the Mormon Church's vast genealogical library in Salt Lake City. If you are researching purely in the UK, a CD ROM player is not a very high priority yet, because little or no information is available for purchase on CD. There is however a lot of very useful data held on CD, that is not available to buy, but is available for our use in **FamilySearch™**. This is a vast database available at many of the LDS Family History Centres, which is stored on a collection of CD ROMs. This is a suite of data accessed from the Family Search program which includes :

The IGI (International Genealogical Index) - an alphabetical index of mainly births, christenings and marriages, taken from original records and submitted genealogy studies, quoting references to the original source.

Ancestral File - a database of family trees and family groups, submitted by any researcher.

USA Social Security Death Index - covering deaths mainly from 1935-95, with useful address information.

USA Military Index - covering the American servicemen and women who died in Korea and Vietnam

Family History Library catalogue - literally a catalogue of all the records on microfiche, CD ROM, microfilm, books documents etc held in the Utah library. It is searchable in many ways, including: locality, surname, subject etc.

The IGI is very useful in this form and individual researchers can download large chunks of it, as well as information from the other CD's, onto floppy disks to search at leisure in their own homes. The data is copied using FamilySearch, from the CD ROM onto a holding file and then transferred to a floppy disk. When you use the system to download IGI data, make sure that you search for Individuals, Marriages and Parents and check the addendum files if appropriate too, to make sure you get all the entries. An hour spent on their computer could provide days of later research, but the program is run on a PC, and your Mac may not recognise PC disks and data, so you need to discover how to set about transferring the data between these two radically different machines. This procedure is also useful if you want to exchange data with another researcher who uses a PC.

Reading a PC disk on a Mac

If you put a PC formatted disk into any but the latest of Mac computers, you will get a message saying something to the effect that "this is not a Macintosh disk do you want to initialize it?" and if you tell it to go ahead you will get a blank, freshly formatted Macintosh disk and your PC data will be lost forever! Macintosh computers since the advent of the Superdrive, have always been able to import and export data to and from PC formatted disks. Many people may not be aware that they have this facility, because it is contained in a little program lurking on one of their system disks and may not even be loaded onto the computer's hard disk. This program, called "Apple File Exchange", is the key to importing and manipulating data from the FamilySearch program as well as reading various files from other PC sources. It is not perhaps the most user friendly program, as it works similarly to the Font/DA Mover that was needed to install and remove fonts before the advent of Apple's operating System 7. If you are lucky enough to own one of the latest Macs though, you may have a Control Panel called "PC Exchange", which recognises the PC disk and mounts it as if it were a Macintosh one, making life very much easier.

Unless your machine has PC Exchange installed and switched on, the first problem is to make the machine recognise the fact that this is a disk containing information, and not a candidate for re-formatting.

Find the program called "Apple File Exchange", contained in the "Apple File Exchange Folder". If you are in the Finder with no files open, use the FIND FILE command to look for it on the hard disk. If you cannot find it, examine the directories on your original system disks to find it and copy the folder onto your hard disk. Once you have found the program, proceed as follows:

1. Locate the "Apple File Exchange" icon with the cursor and double click to launch it. It will look similar to the illustration (Figure 16), but with the right hand panel blank.
2. Now using the NEW FOLDER button, set up and name a new folder to store the translated PC files in, unless you just want to throw them in with the rest of your files! Or use the DRIVE and OPEN buttons to navigate to an existing folder where you want to store the data.
3. Insert your PC disk into the drive, the Mac will now accept and read the disk, displaying a directory of its contents in the right hand window.

4. Select the PC file you want to transfer and use the translate button to transfer the data to Macintosh format. When the file has been copied, it's name will appear in your new folder in the left hand window. Repeat the operation until all your files have been transferred.

If you are transferring data from the Mac onto a PC floppy disk, the operation is simply carried out in reverse, and the program will tell you how many bytes you have selected and how much space is left on the disk you are filling, to make sure the file will fit the remaining disk space.

A default format for translation is automatically used, but if you are translating text, then you can decide how RETURNS, TABS etc are treated during transfer, by using the pull down menus which appear on the menu bar when the disk is inserted. You can find out more about the translation options from "About Apple File Exchange" in the Apple menu.

You can use the program to format disks for the PC, as well as to translate your Macintosh files onto it. It is a straightforward operation, put in an unformatted disk and the computer will ask you what the disk should be formatted as, again you should find further details in your computer's user guide.

If you have the "PC Exchange" control panel in the system folder, and it is switched on, the Mac will immediately recognise the disk and read it as if it were a native Macintosh disk. The translation of data is automatic and files may be downloaded or copied to the disk by "drag and drop", just as if it was a normal Macintosh formatted one. By opening the Control Panels folder in the Apple menu and selecting the PC Exchange icon, you will get a preferences box which will allow you to use the MS-DOS file name suffix to allocate which program will handle the document, set it to send files to your word-processor, but don't use this to

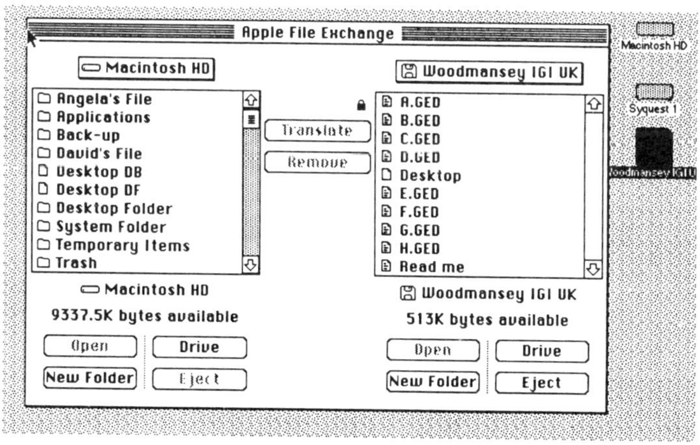

Figure 16 Using Apple File Exchange allows you to transfer files from a PC formatted disk (in the right hand window) to your Hard disk (Left hand window) Files are highlighted and individually transferred.

automatically allocate database files.

Having transferred the data files to your hard disk, you now need to be able to access the data. The Family Search program will transfer data in ASCII (which is basically a simple text file), and GEDCOM 2.0 and 2.1 (which is a specially formatted text file). The 2.0 and 2.1 refer to the versions of PAF that use the formats, not the version of GEDCOM, It is useful to download the holding file as an ASCll file and again as a GEDCOM 2.1 unless you have access to a PC as well as a Mac. You can use a PC shareware utility to convert the GEDCOM 2.1 output to Database, DBF format, but you will need to do this on someone's PC with a program such as GIPSI or IGI READ. If you own one of the very latest Macs with a PC emulator program you could actually do the conversion on the Mac, but most of us will have to find a friendly PC owner.

I found a problem with some of the long address fields which were converted from the American Social Security Death Index using GIPSI. These had been truncated as they were converted, leaving in some cases only half of the address. This was not immediately obvious to someone who was not very familiar with the layout of American addresses, many of which seem incredibly short for such a large country anyway. However the most important search variables of names, dates and states, were not altered, so the files were still usable for searching, but the original ASCll file had to be consulted to get the full addresses in many cases.

Other transfers

You may also receive data from various word processors, databases or spreadsheets used by other researchers using PCs, and wish to get the information onto your computer. It is not very difficult, once you know how!

Word-processor/Text documents : Many types of document can be opened with a standard word processor, as a text document. I usually use WriteNow 4 to do this, as it has a wider range of word-processor translations than my integrated package, but any word-processor will do.

If you try to open one of your translated files in the same way as one of your word-processor files, by double clicking on it, you will probably be told that it cannot be opened because "the application that created it is not available" and the Mac may offer to open it in TeachText. However unless it is a very small file, TeachText will not be able to open it and you will have to use a different route.

Open your word-processor program and select OPEN from the FILE menu and use the DESKTOP and OPEN buttons to find the foreign file you want to open, select the file and click OPEN, your word-processor should now open the file.

You will be able to read the contents of the transferred file. If it was an ASCII file or word-processor file that your program contained the proper translator for, the document will appear relatively normal, although it may look a little odd, with extra line spaces and short lines. If the document was produced on a word processor and your package does not have the proper translator for the format, some of the layout and formatting codes may be thrown in amongst the text, and some files may seem totally up the creek! I recently opened a complex 2 page document written in Word

6 for Windows, it opened as a 50+ page document on my word-processor, because of all the layout codes and font changes! You can try and use your Find and Replace function to tidy up the document, but it was not designed to cope with this problem and does not always work too well.

Another problem you may come across is not having the correct fonts installed on your computer, and you may get a mass of empty squares or black bars if your program uses the wrong font. Don't immediately despair and think that you cannot read the document, but try selecting all the text and change it to one of your standard fonts.

ASCII or Text files downloaded from the FamilySearch program are neatly formatted and may be printed out our browsed through on the screen. You cannot sort the information, but you can use your word-processors find and replace facility as a key name or word search.

GEDCOM files: These are specially formatted text files and can also be opened and read with a word-processor, useful if you suspect some data may have been lost when you transfer a file. The GEDCOM files can of course be opened and imported into a family history program which uses that file transfer format. This is usually a straightforward procedure and will be detailed in your user manual. Save the files as GEDCOM 2.1 (actually GEDCOM version4) when you are using family search, as this is the format used by the latest genealogy programs.

Don't put GEDCOM data direct into your current family history datafile, GEDCOM files from the IGI opened in a family history program, will give you many three person family groups and a lot of duplications, so it is better to put them into a new family file, or into an ordinary database program to do your research, as the search and sort facilities are often better and quicker.

Database files : When you are copying large chunks of data, such as the IGI, to put into a database, you need to change the Family Search information into Database Format first, using a utility program like GIPSI or IGIREAD run on a PC. There are plenty of PC owners around, so you should not have any difficulty getting a friend or fellow member of a family history society to convert your file for you. DBF files are only visible on most Apple Macintosh Database menus **after** they have been imported and converted. This is unlike foreign word processor files, which usually appear on menus even when created by a program you don't own.

The following is the procedure I have adopted to import DBF 3 formatted data, converted from IGI GEDCOM files, into Claris FileMaker Pro. A similar procedure should work with other databases, including those found in integrated packages.

If you are using PC Exchange, it is important that you do not allow it to tag the DBF files with the name of your database as you copy them onto the hard disk. Open it's control panel and make sure you haven't got it set to tag DOS files marked DBF directly for your database. If they are tagged, they cannot be opened, and you will get a message to say they are corrupted when you try to import them. Users of Apple File Exchange will not have this problem.

Importing records into a database such as Claris FileMaker Pro, firstly requires the setting up of a NEW database containing all the necessary fields. You could import into an existing database, but if you do make sure you have a back-up copy first. Setting up the correct fields is a bit of a chicken and egg situation, as you probably don't know what fields were used originally; and until the program allows you to Import, you cannot check what fields are used in your transferred data file. The following method works with FileMaker; other databases will tend to be similar.

On opening a new database, the program first requires you to set up the fields, before it will let you do anything else. As you probably don't know what fields are required, set up just one field with any name you like (see Figure 17) and click DONE, this will satisfy the program and allow you to proceed to the next step. Now select IMPORT from the FILE menu and navigate to your DBF file, which you have already converted from PC format using "Apple File Exchange", or direct from the PC formatted floppy disk if you have "PC Exchange". Open the file and a window will appear with two columns (as in Figure 18), one will contain a list of fields in the database you want to import, make a note of these field names, the other column will contain the name of the solitary field on your new database. Now click CANCEL, and go back to the SELECT menu and select DEFINE FIELDS, you can now set up and name all the fields you require, deleting the original field if it wasn't appropriately named. When you have finished setting up all the required fields, click DONE and

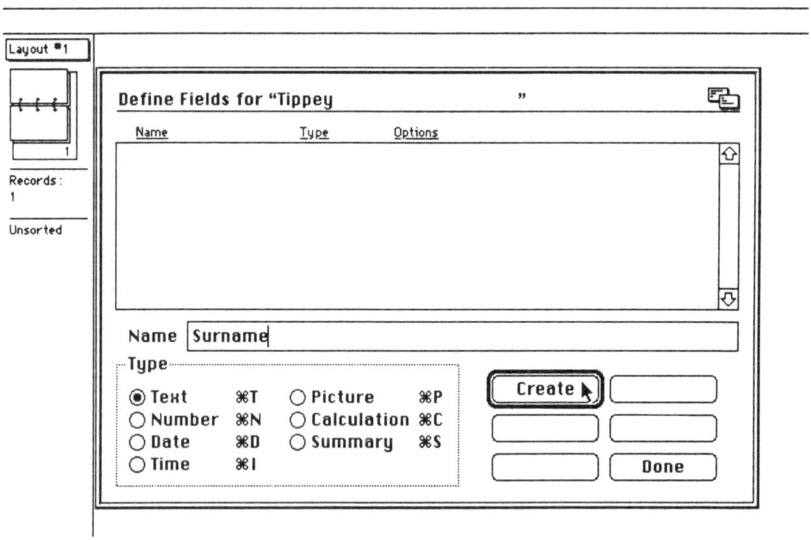

Figure 17 When you open a new database in a program like Filemaker Pro, you cannot Import information straight into it without setting up the fields to accept the information first. Define one field name (in this case Surname) to keep the program happy then click Done.

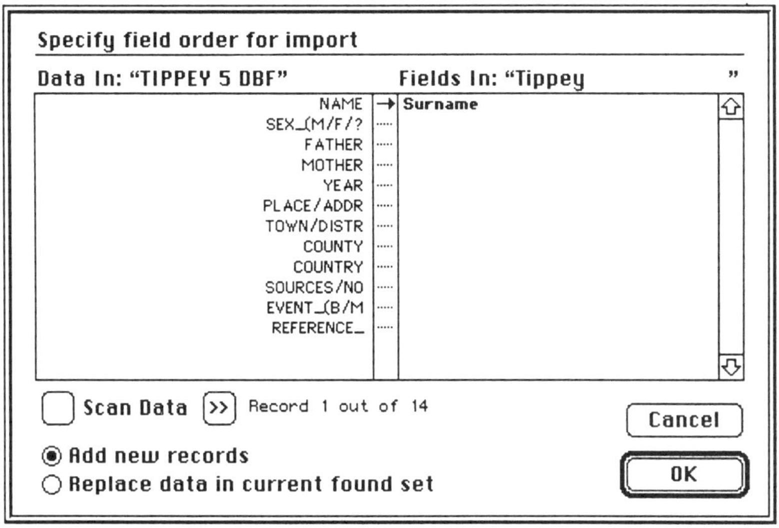

Figure 18 Having created a database with one field, "SURNAME" you can use the Import command to find out what other fields you need to set up before finally Importing your data.

then select IMPORT again from the FILE menu. When the import window appears this time, you should have a matching set of field names in each column. You can re-arrange which information is put where, if the lists of fields are not in the same order. When you have checked where all the information is going click OK and the data will be imported into your new database. You can now browse, search and work with the data as normal.

Using your own computer to store and search IGI and other FamilySearch information is a far better option than using the microfiche IGI at the local library, which is pretty tedious, especially when someone mis-filed the fiche you want! You can download the sections you need, from all around the world, for the cost of a new disk, and then browse them at your leisure, in your own home, anytime.

One other possible source for data that you can use on your own computer is the ESRC Data Archive at the University of Essex, Wivenhoe Park, Colchester, Essex CO4 3SQ. They hold various material of interest to family and local historians including the 2% sample of the 1851 Census of Great Britain and many interesting local data holdings, however the access and charges structure is rather inscrutable (you have to fill out 4 forms before they will even tell you what the data will cost you), which will put most people off.

Chapter 6 : Pictures and documents

Many family history programs will allow you to access digitised photographs and even include them on family trees. Many other programs such as word processing or drawing and paint programs will also let you use stored images too. Of course you are not limited to photographs, you can scan drawings, maps, and old documents too. Firstly though you need to convert your photograph or whatever into data usable by the computer. You can view very high resolution images on your monitor, but the quality of the images printed out in your documents and reports will depend on the quality of your printer. To get passable reproduction you need a printer with a resolution of at least 300 dpi (dots per inch), which includes most inkjets, although an inkjet or laser printer of 600 dpi+ resolution will give far superior results. Results from laser printers are usually better than those from inkjets, as these often show a faint stripe in areas of solid colour.

Scanners : The photograph is converted to a graphic data file using a scanner. Unless you visualise needing one a great deal, a scanner would be a fairly expensive piece of equipment to add to your computer. They range in price from a few hundred pounds to thousands for the drum scanners used by graphics studios. The cheapest option may be a hand held version, which is simply dragged over the document or photograph. Unfortunately there is now only one hand held scanner that I know of, produced for the Mac, and the price is quite steep. The cheapest A4 flat-bed colour scanners suitable for our use cost between £400-500, lucky PC owners can buy a hand scanner for under £100, which would give results good enough to use with a 300 dpi printer! If you opt to buy a scanner, try and make sure you get one of the deals which include either Photoshop LE or Color It software included, so that you can manipulate and re-touch your scans.

If you own a fax, you can now get a little interface which will allow you to use it as a scanner, but I don't know what the quality would be like. I hope it's better than the printed faxes I get!

With the appropriate OCR software (Optical Character Recognition), you can also use your scanner to input typed or printed documents directly into your computer as text, which you can then treat like any other word processing document. This feature can be useful if you want to include extracts from books into your family history, by saving many hours typing.

Scanning Services : Help is at hand though, scanning services are becoming much more common and some are regularly advertised in "Family Tree Magazine".

Many of these services will be using PCs though, and to use the resulting scan on the Mac it usually has to be converted into PICT format, although some programs can also use images in TIFF format. PICT is the format the Mac uses to transfer pictures and graphics between applications, via the clipboard, so this format is usually chosen for ease of handling.

The scanning bureau may use a Mac though, in which case you can get your photographic scan saved as a PICT file, but if they use a PC the file may have to be saved as a TIFF. The person who does my scans for me scans the image into Photoshop and then saves the file as a TIFF (Photoshop has options for Mac and PC format TIFFs). I then open the file using the free version of Color IT that came with MacFormat issue 31, where I can retouch and crop the image, before saving it as a PICT, which can be handled by my other programs. Some draw and paint packages enable you to read both PICT and TIFF files and then save them in PICT format.

A cheap shareware program called "Graphic Converter 2.1.2" can convert most formats found in graphics files (even some of the strange ones you may find on the Internet) and it will also allow you to do some simple editing, like cropping and rotating the image. It can be obtained from a shareware supplier, although a copy was included in the cover disk of MacFormat May 1995.

Scan Specification : When you specify how your scan is done, it is not just the file format that you need to know. If you have the image scanned at too high a resolution, the files will be massive and the resolution higher than you can use on your screen or printer. It is useful to have two scans done for each picture, 70-100 dpi (dots per inch) to display on your monitor and one at 200-300 dpi for your printer, or higher if you have a better printer or want to do considerable re-touching. Some re-touching programs, including Photoshop, will allow you to re-save images at different resolutions.

B&W photographs should be scanned as "Greyscale", and colour photographs or old B&W photos with hand coloured re-touching, scanned as 8 bit colour (256 colours) for standard colour monitors. 32 bit colour (thousands of colours) is available, but usually only used for the highest quality work. If you want to do any major retouching on images, have them scanned at a higher resolution (600-1200 dpi), to allow you to zoom in and re-touch more accurately and easily. I find that TIFF files tend to give better quality prints than PICT files on my ink-jet printer, I don't know why, but it is not always possible to incorporate them in other documents, as you can with a PICT.

Enhancing the image : Oncc you have your photograph on the computer, you may like to enhance it by retouching or editing it. You can get rid of creases and scratches, crop, change scale, increase contrast and all manner of other adjustments, if you have a suitable program.

Photoshop is the benchmark, a professional, photo re-touching application. A cut down version without colour separation facilities, which you probably wouldn't need, is sold as Photoshop LE, and often bundled with scanner purchases.

Color-It is a fairly new package to the UK market, an older, but still very good version of it, already mentioned, was given free with MacFormat December 1995 issue, if you can still get the back issue, it's well worth having.

There are various other suitable programs including the B&W only GrayStation and it's sister program ColourStation, and again GrayStation was given free with MacFormat in the August 1994 issue. There is also a comprehensive Freeware program called NIH Image vers.1.55, originally developed for enhancing medical brain scans, it comes with a fairly comprehensive manual on disc and will accept photoshop plug-ins. You can get a copy from a shareware supplier and there is no registration fee.

For photographic quality prints of your re-touched images, they will have to be printed on one of the high quality, 1200 or 1800 dpi machines at a print and scanning bureau. The files are likely to be anything up to 10Mb or more in size though, so you will have difficulty in taking your files to the bureau unless you have a removable hard disk drive, like a Syquest, or can split the program over several floppy disks using a disk utility program.

Photo CD ROMs : There is another way to get pictures onto your computer, which doesn't involve owning or having direct access to a scanner, providing you have a CD ROM drive.

Kodak have a service for transferring photographs straight onto CD, the service is available from Boots and some Kodak processing shops. This means you can re-photograph your family album or family documents and take photographs of buildings and places with your camera and then take the film along and have it transferred onto a CD.

The CD will store about 100 images from a 35mm camera. There is an initial charge of about £7 for the CD and you can have your film transferred to it for about 60p per image. The CDs are multi-session, which means you can take them back again and have more images added.

Most CD ROM driver software now supports these Kodak Photo CDs, and many paint /re-touching programs can import images directly from the disk. The photo CD treats all images as being colour, so you will have to import B&W images as greyscale. The images may be imported at different magnifications too.

This is a is a much cheaper option for using pictures than buying a scanner, because you can buy a double speed CD ROM drive for less than a third of the cost of the cheapest flat-bed scanners.

Chapter 7 : The Internet, CompuServe, etc.

From Dusty Archives to Cyberspace :

There is one more use for your computer which may help forward your genealogical research, purchase a modem and connect yourself to the Internet. Unfortunately, most people find the Internet (Net) and the World Wide Web (Web or WWW), shrouded in more mystery than MS DOS, they are completely baffled by it. This is despite the fact that they keep reading about it and are constantly assured by others, that it is the best thing to happen to communications since Marconi!

The best way to find out about the Net is to find someone who is already using it to demonstrate the system and show you just what use it is for a genealogist. Another alternative is to visit a cyber-cafe, they seem to be the up and coming thing in the larger cities and there you can get an introduction to the Net for about the cost of a trip to the cinema. Or you could read David Hawgood's "Internet for Genealogy", but as you are already here, reading this chapter may help clarify things a little, but there is nothing like hands-on experience.

The Internet, what is it?

Basically it is a giant network of computers covering the world, it is built up of smaller networks of linked computers, each sharing files and information and able to communicate with each other. Networks are run by governments, universities, large companies etc and also the commercial on-line service providers like the well known Compuserve, CIX , Demon and PIPEX.

Each network holds information, databases etc., and between them they cover an infinite variety of topics. The networks can communicate with each other to exchange information, using the equivalent of the International telephone system. Data is not usually accessed directly from the source network, but is routed through various networks until it reaches it's final destination.

No one actually owns the Internet, only their own small part of it, but it is over-seen by the Internet Society, who appoint a group who decide on the communication rules which make it workable.

The Internet Society estimate that around 30 million people had Internet access to around 4 million host computers in 1995, and the Net is doubling in size each year!

WWW?

The World Wide Web could be described as something akin to a Tourist Information system for the Net, helping you navigate the Internet, finding information more easily.

It contains pages of information accessed by a program called a Web browser, you pick a topic that interests you and a web page will be displayed. This page will link you quite seamlessly, via specially highlighted words or buttons, to other associated files, which may be on a site on the other side of the world. These pages may not only contain text, but also pictures and video footage too.

The WWW helps you "surf the Net" easily, just a mouse click enabling you to skip around the world, without even realising it. The bias is still very heavily American,

but a very useful set of web pages for UK researchers to find is the UK + Ireland Genealogy page, whose Uniform Resource Locator address is:
http://midas.ac.uk/genuki/

Many sites accessed from web pages contain files and programs that you can download as well as read, where you can get utility programs and up-dates, and it is even possible to publish your own Web Page.

Email

This is the one facility that has potential uses in any family, whether or not you are into family history. Electronic mail gives you the facility to send and receive letters etc. to and from anyone in the world with an Email address. The mail can be collected on the other side of the world virtually instantaneously and it will cost you the same as a local telephone call. You can also attach things to your Email messages, such as pictures or GEDCOM files. You can send an Email to one person or many different ones at the same time. Mailing lists are Email based discussion groups, a useful one for genealogists is ROOTS-L. To get information about this (from an automatic message handler), send an email with any subject, and with message content: **info ROOTS-L** to email address: **listserv@mail.eworld.com**
Emails are automatically posted to all members who have subscribed to that particular mailing list (this is free and really consists of adding your Email address to the group's address list) You can post your reaction to the messages either directly to the inquirer or to the whole forum. Unlike general Email messages posted to newsgroups and discussion forums, personal Email is private and is stored in your own personal directory for collection.

Usenet

This is the system used for public Email group discussions, where you are able to enter into discussion with other people sharing your interests. There are groups discussing just about any conceivable subject, including genealogy, and the debate can be quite lively. Special newsreader software allows you to post messages to a group or call up the messages posted by others.

A word of warning is required here though; you must remember that you are communicating with real people not computers and as well as being helpful, they may be rude and intolerant, especially if you ask what is to them a stupid question. It is better to observe the dialogue for a while before you join in, and make the most of the FAQs (frequently asked questions) which are listed.

Bulletin Boards

The cheapest way to connect your computer to a source of genealogical interest is to call up a bulletin board. Some of these specialise in Family history research and they provide a message service for you to contact and receive mail from other researchers using the same board and may allow you to have an Internet Email address. CompuServe and CIX are sophisticated versions of a bulletin board. They also have various files, indexes etc that you can use. The cost to you is simply the cost of the phone call, it's at normal phone rates though, so don't spend hours trawling the Foreign boards, join the Internet.

CompuServe

Often confused with the Internet itself by the uninitiated, CompuServe is a service provider, really an advanced bulletin board. They offer high quality services, backed by custom written software, to make it easy to use. The Email system is very good and you have access to the Internet.

Information sent over the Internet is broken up into packets, which may come to your computer via different routes, one of the frustrations of using the Internet at a busy time is that you may lose your connection or get an incomplete set of data. One of the advantages of using a large service provider like CompuServe is that you are more likely to get reliable connections, because they are in a position to pay for more lines.

What Do I Need?

Besides your computer and a phone line, you will need a modem and various pieces of software to allow you to use the different facilities. Modems are becoming much cheaper, and it will pay you to buy one of the faster ones, as it will save you money in line charges. The speed of data is measured in bits per second, and modem speeds are expressed as a baud rate(bps). The higher the baud rate the faster the modem and the quicker the files will transfer. Faster modems are more expensive, but the price is also effected by the various data compression and checking facilities it can cope with. Modems are available with speeds of 9,600, 14,400 and 28,800 bps, and if you buy a fax modem you can send faxes from your computer too. Modems usually come supplied with some software, and you may find you already have some in an integrated program like Claris or Microsoft Works. To join the internet you need to get access to the system, you do this through a company called a Provider, the charges and facilities vary from one to another, so it is worth checking out what you are getting included in your monthly subscription and how much the extra access time costs.

Providers include :-
CityScape - 01223 566950
CIX, Compulink Information Exchange - 0181 390 8446
CompuServe - 01492 641961
Demon - 0181 349 0063

Genealogical information on-line

I know of four smaller Bulletin Boards catering for genealogists in the UK, which would be worth exploring for sources of information and like-minded researchers:

French Connection - Fareham, 01329 239101
Jacob's Well - Bristol, 0117 9686786
Quills Queries - Lindfield, 01444 483769
Ridjek Thome - Emsworth, 01243 370249

If you join CompuServe look for the Roots directory which is a library containing programs, articles, book reviews, pictures and all manner of items of genealogical interest.

There are various genealogical discussion forums available for Internet users, plus useful programs and interesting documents to download. The discussion forums allow you to ask general questions or ones that are specific to your research, look out for the ROOTS-L mailing list mentioned above. You will also find details of new and old publications of interest to family historians and find people offering information and help from books , documents etc. that they hold.

The web page UK + Ireland Genealogy is set up and it's contents are constantly being added to, a useful place to check out if your research takes you to a fresh area of the country. Actual data for UK researchers is really only just starting to become available via the Internet, however if you are researching ancestors in America and Canada you will find plenty of useful sites to explore.

Bibliography

Parts of the material in this book have appeared before in articles by David Tippey:

Computers in Genealogy Vol 5 no 8, Dec 1995
Review of Reunion 4 for Macintosh, p357
Review of Gene 4.1 for Macintosh, p363.
Computers in Genealogy Vol 5 No 9, Mar 1996, p398
PAF 2.1 for Macintosh
Family Tree Magazine Jan 1996, p28.
FamilySearch and other PC data on the Macintosh
Family Tree Magazine Dec 1995, p28. Gene 4.1, shareware for the Macintosh.
Family Tree Magazine Mar 1995. p28.
Genealogy programs for the Macintosh computer; an overview of the UK market.